# THE NEW
# ZONE SYSTEM MANUAL
## WHITE · ZAKIA · LORENZ

Since Seeing depends on Craftsmanship
and Craftsmanship depends on Seeing,
then some part of photography depends
on balancing both.
The Art?

First Printing, January 1976
Second Printing, October 1976
Third Printing, April 1977
Fourth Printing, January 1978

International Standard Book
Number 0-87100-100-4
Library of Congress Catalog Card
Number 75-428-77

Printed in U.S.A.

Type set and printed by
Morgan Press Incorporated, Dobbs Ferry, N.Y.

# Table of Contents

"Some of the young photographers today enter photography where I leave off. My "grandchildren" astound me. What I worked for they seem to be born with. So I wonder where *Their* affirmations of Spirit will lead. My wish for them is that their unfolding proceeds to fullness of Spirit, however astonishing or anguished their lives."

Minor White
*Mirrors, Messages Manifestations*

# The Efficacy of Craft and Vision

The most distinctive feature of this present work, under the combined authorship of Minor White, Richard Zakia and Peter Lorenz, is that it provides the reader with the most comprehensive discussion of the zone system yet published. Through their combined talents, they have been able to articulate not just simply a methodology, but a very challenging interplay and clarification of the interdependence of craft as it can relate to vision.

One should not consider the system as an intrusion in any way upon a visual response. The declarative or expressive position of the photographer in relation to the photographic medium should be based upon the fullest understanding of all the ingredients essential to his craft. The proposition is one of vision, and in an interesting way vision can ultimately extend craft, and it is even possible for a sense of craft to aid in the extension of vision. When technical confidence and not just simply competence is the issue, the photographer will not reveal in his work distinctly separate talents—craft with the absence of vision, or vision with the absence of craft—but rather an appropriate fusion. Union of technique and imagination will be an important basis for his expressive concerns. It will be this confidence that will enable him to engage freely and spontaneously.

As I interpret the authors' position, the system is intended to generate a symbiotic relationship between response and pictured response. The system is in effect syntactical and a wide latitude for personal interpretation is inherently possible. In effect, the system helps to reveal and clarify the syntax and should not be considered an end in itself. This position has been consistently maintained by Minor White. In his original zone system manual, published in 1961, he stated:

> Any artist or craftsman uses mental tools to guide himself as he molds materials with his physical tools. Some of these concepts are codified, such as color systems or harmonics. In photography such concepts have their counterparts in optics, that pertains to the image projection qualities of lenses; and sensitometry, that is the study of the effect of light intensities on photographic emulsions. Man's mental tools are in the nature of approaches or working philosophies such as the Memory Recall school of acting. In photography, Ansel Adams was the first to codify how experienced photographers have, in effect, always used their materials.
>
> Adams first called it the Zone System of Planned Photography. Criticism has been aimed at anything so intellectual as planning a photograph, by persons who fear that the slighest trace of thinking will spoil their spontaneity. There is some truth in their fears—as any young musician learning scales will testify. Legion are the "photographers" who can raise a camera spontaneously to their intuitive eye—and fail to produce a print. The parallel still holds between word-men who breathe poetry into the restrictions of the sonnet and those picture-men who breathe spontaneous life into planned photographs.

The zone system provides an exceptional method of revealing and understanding the syntax of photography. The establishment of meaningful patterns to communicate thought and feeling is the province of language, be it visual or verbal. The task of the photographer is to develop a personal vocabulary, a cogent and cognitive reflection of his expressed concerns through the photographs he makes.

—Nathan Lyons
Visual Studies Workshop

# Authors' Preface

**Photographic chemistry is changing.**
**Equipment is in the throes of automation.**
**Weston exposure meters are phasing out.**
**As foolproofing advances, Contrast-Control diminishes.**
**But the principles of sensitometry upon which the Zone System stands, remain firm.**
**And visualization always has the creative power to accommodate whatever changes are ahead.**

Believing that three authors might reflect the present nature of a zone system more clearly than one, a trained sensitometrist (Zakia, under 50), a free-lance instructor of zone system workshops (Lorenz, under 30) and an exhibition photographer (White, under 70) joined forces. Long before we started to work together we had separately concluded that efforts to simplify the system are wasted. We believe that only clarification, rather than simplification, can steer us through the complexities of the photographic process that an introduction to the zone system soon reveals. Therefore we aim to clarify its mechanics in this book; its alchemy we leave to another.

Persons intrigued by the system are led, unsuspectingly, to examine some of photography's many complexities. In their attempts to clarify photography and system to themselves, some persons write books. The present authors are no exception. Zakia makes his approach through sensitometry because science and light-sensitive materials are his realm of involvement; Lorenz stresses calibration because he loves well-crafted images; White concentrates on previsualization because he can not think in numbers.

Each of us presents a different "picture" of the Zone System: the general view, the view from the calibration side and the sensitometrist's viewpoint, in that order. The "pictures" overlap, but in a way that helps explain what went before. Moving from generalities to specifics forced a change from simplicity to complexity. In the beginning at least we were able to keep in mind visual minded photographers who are bewildered by numbers and who shrink from "candles-per-square-foot".

People ask, "What is this Zone System?"

It explains little if anything to say that essentially the system amounts to practical sensitometry combined with sensitized vision; or to put it in the negative, say that *without* visualization the system is an over complicated set of finger exercises. Or to point out, in a positive tone again, that visualization mixed with zone system sensitometry can evolve into a way of life, much as flour and water when heated turn into bread. Bread that

2

nourishes each of us according to our needs. Little is explained when we say that photography's unique physical problem is to neatly couple exposure control to development control in the endless struggle with subject contrast; or to add that it is all done by visualization, a zoned gray scale, standardized processing, and a calibrated luminance meter. Is anything clarified when we say that the problems characteristic of photography may be symbolized by the astrological sign, Pisces—two fish tied together swimming in opposite directions? However, a promise is made when we say that the system offers still photographers who are willing to work, control of the controls.

These unexplained statements are true enough, but any understanding of them will only be reached by exploring them.

Practice makes us believe that visualization is of the essence when creativity relates to photography. Photographers can visualize before making the exposure, before printing the negative, and visualize how viewers may respond before showing the print. Once they have previsualized they may revisualize at any time they wish and for whatever reason. However it is used, visualization sparks all zone system activity: the system as process, calibration and sensitometry. All three support the creativity that visualization brings to photography.

### Calibrations and Sensitomery

At the head of the system stands the luminance meter: measurement-taker, expediter and guardian. But meters must be calibrated to measure luminances in zones. Consequently calibration and material testing is an on-going part of a systemized photographer's career; because it keeps all variables under control, connects photographer to medium, makes visualizing possible

and effective. In brief it gives to a photographer's imagination a "keyboard" to photography's gray (tone) and color (hue) possibilities. As we experience calibration, it will be easy to comprehend that calibrated exposure meters also guard the heart of the system.

Harder for photographers to grasp is the place of *sensitometry* in making photographs. Let's dwell on this for a moment. Between the art of photography and the science of photography rumor has it that a wedding will take place any day. No one is sure which is groom and which is bride. As we worked on the book we wondered if we might find ourselves minister—inadvertently, of course. What we did find surprised us: sensitometrists say that graphs and curves are pictures of photographs and equivalent to photographs, if not actually photographs! What was more, we found that a sensitometrist poring over his graphs and a cameraman poring over his photographs are both linked to the creative. Though sensitometrists favor facsimile reproduction and pictorialists lean toward personal interpretation, each seeks to predict results, the one by mathematics, the other by intuition. Each exercises creative imagination in much the same way, by some form of visualization.

Our aim for some time now has been to encourage the incorporation of sensitometrists' views about materials with photographers' views about vision. Pioneer photographers never knew the dichotomy of manufacturer and operator; now the two live in different worlds. We would draw them together again for mutual gain. When we notice that the trend toward automation tends to further separate photo scientist from photographer, we feel a little lonely.

Regarding the text, the material has been compressed enough so that we suggest three readings: first, skim to gain orientation; second, make notes for understanding and reference; and third, use camera, film, and developer.

We close with a warning about letting the practice of this system drift into mechanical ritual. At first, newness of ideas and routines will keep the practice lively. Eventually it is likely to atrophy into mechanical gestures, despite New Year's resolutions every day. So, invent new questions frequently as the years accumulate. Two model approaches follow: the photographer may apply variations of them whenever stagnation seems imminent.

**1.** After grasping an intellectual meaning of some one zone, for example, let heart inform you about its emotional meaning. Still later let body-understanding inform you about the sensory nature of all ten zones, one at a time, as you feel ready.

**2.** When a formal, zone system meaning of the term "normal print" has been digested, begin to ask how Normal relates to photography's psychology; how it relates to an aesthetic sense, to your emotional experience of normalcy, and so on, seeing ever wider relationships.

The form of the model for revivifying questions follows: first introduce some phase or item into yourself by way of the mind; then expand the experience of it through both the emotional and sensory sides—through the wholeness of your self; think up new leading questions to activate both sensory and emotional participation.

## Acknowledgements

**W**e are all indebted to Ansel Adams for his encouragement and advice as the work progressed, and wish to take this opportunity to express our gratitude. Working together brought about new understandings of familiar problems; for this we are deeply grateful.

We observe the passing of the Weston Electrical Instrument Company with misgivings and profound regret.

**Richard Zakia** wishes especially to thank Hollis Todd, for his close scrutiny of the manuscript; George DeWolfe, John Dowdell, Sue Martin for their help in this work; and Lois for her constant encouragement.

**Peter Lorenz** wishes to thank Carolyn Sagov, Curt Lamb and Helen McMullen who supported and encouraged his first teaching in zone system workshops in 1973; Art Robbins for his calibration work with D-76; and Harry DeRham who continues to be a source of inspiration for his work.

**Minor White** welcomes this moment to acknowledge and express his gratitude to a host of sources and writers, students and assistants, typists and proofreaders. He wants to thank Lisa DeLima, Steve Slesinger and Kelly Cross for yeoman duty at typewriter and blue pencil.

# Overview of a Zone System*

Perhaps the most important thing to be learned from practicing the zone system is the concept of previsualization. The word itself means simply "to see ahead of time". Isn't that what the whole picture making process seems to be about? You go to make a picture and try to *make* it "come-out" like some notion in your head. We all realize that we can't take a scene which is multidimensional by nature and produce an exact copy of it in a two-dimensional photograph. We realize too that a black and white picture is not the same as the subject which is actually colored. We cannot reproduce exactly the scene which is before our camera; we can only come up with an approximation. Nevertheless the photograph can and does have a life of its own!

If you understand what photographic materials can do, you can learn to form a mental image of the finished photograph *before* you actually trip the shutter.

Your mental picture may, of course, be one of many things. You may have a mental picture which is absolutely unlike the scene before you. Your mental conception may be a composite of two or three or more pictures; it may be sharp or fuzzy. This is where your individuality comes in. Knowledge of photography allows the photographer to make successful photographs from these mental images.

With the Zone System, we first previsualize, plan a strategy of exposure and development and produce a print to make the previsualized image a reality. The success of the process is dependent upon *how well the print matches the mental pic-ture, not how well it matches the original scene.* This idea should not be too surprising as you've been doing it all along without realizing it. Photographers seldom return with a print to the site of the photograph just to check and see how well it "came out". Zone system previsualization intensifies this same process.

The first step after previsualization is exposure of the film. With the zone system there is no such thing as over- and underexposure, or over- and underdevelopment either, except by accident. Granted that our exposures will vary, therefore some negatives will look thin and others dense, but we will have made them that way on purpose. Thus the thin negatives and the dense ones, since they were made that way with a certain kind of print in mind, are not improperly exposed. Any exposure is correct if it produces the negative best suited to materialize your mental picture.

Mastery of exposure is dependent upon our knowledge of the film, camera, and meter used. Experience in a zone system reduces the problems of exposure to reflex actions which aid in "capturing" that previsualized mental picture.

Likewise, development is no longer to be considered in terms of "over" and "under". Through a simple set of tests you will learn the effects of a range of developments upon your own film. Knowing how your film reacts to different developments will enable you to pick the one to get your mental picture on paper the way you "saw" it in your head and felt it in your heart. Any

*Slightly edited from David R. Young's Senior Thesis, Rochester Institute of Technology (1962)

development is correct if it produces the negative most suited to materialize your mental picture.

When you get to printing the film you should have a negative which was exposed and developed to the appropriate contrast *within a zone* to produce the print you previsualized. If this is the case, printing becomes quite simple: it's easy to make the kind of prints you want from negatives that are integral parts of the process. Of course you will vary slightly (within a zone) print exposure, development, dodging, and burning-in to put the finishing touches on your previsualized image. That is general practice. With the problems of printing thus drastically reduced, you are free to get down to serious work.

After producing a finished print we generally take the time to evaluate how close we came to accomplishing the task of recording the original previsualized image. This is part of what is called postvisualization. It takes some mental gymnastics, but you'll find them delightful after a bit of practice. What we learn each time prepares us for the next photograph.

Up until this point no one else has seen your first mental picture. It was stuck in your head until you got it into a print on paper. It is much as though you were an author writing a novel. An author usually re-reads his or her manuscript to be sure he has presented the ideas as clearly and concisely as possible. During postvisualization you have a chance to re-read your manuscript to see how well you are communicating your ideas through pictures.

This then is an overview of a zone system. Previsualization is the beginning, control of the process is in the middle, and postvisualization brings the process full circle.

—David R. Young

*Users of the zone system measure contrast of subjects in zones. The word "contrast" is associated with the tonal range from lightest to darkest in either subject or photographic print. To plan photographs by this system "local contrast" is considered together with "overall contrast." Many of the compromises (or "trade-offs," if you prefer that term) are chosen so as to favor some "local contrast."*

*In the picture on the opposite page, the local contrast, measured in zones, of course, on the dark side is the same as the local contrast on the bright side. Each has a contrast of about five zones. To photograph both sides on the same sheet of film, the photographer had to work with an overall contrast of about ten zones.*

Local Contrast ◀──────────────▶◀────────────── Local Contrast ──────────────▶

◀────────────────────── **Overall Contrast** ──────────────────────▶

# Glossary

The word sequence is non-alphabetical. The word sequence has been selected to suggest an outline of the photographic process.

**Luminance:** Light reflected from subjects, meter-measurable and hence "objective".

**Brightness:** Human subjective experience of luminance, hence unmeasurable.

**Luminance Meter:** Instrument for measuring reflected light. When calibrated in zones makes visualization possible and positive.

**Value:** Two meanings adhere: 1) Measurable "grayness" of reflected light, neither hue nor chroma. 2) Unmeasurable qualities of color, texture, and brightness as seen by eye and lens and transfered by visualization and technical procedures to print values.

**Continuous Value Scale:** Gray scale without steps, segments or zones. Typical of photographic materials.

**Zone:** A short segment or area, of local contrast within the greater contrast of an entire gray scale. The intervals are based on an exposure ratio of 1:2. Zone V, for example, represents twice as much exposure as Zone IV and one half as much as Zone VI. The same ratio holds for brightness and luminances. Zone V represents twice as much light reflected from a surface as Zone IV and one half as much as Zone VI, and so on.

The number of Zones in photographic gray scales can vary according to the decision of the photographer. 9 zone, 10 zone or 11 zone scales are considered "Normal."

**Zoned Gray Scale:** A continuous value scale of all the

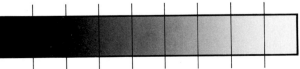

tonalities in a gray scale arbitrarily segmented in stops (1:2 exposure ratios).

**Stepped Gray Scale:** *Symbolic* of the zoned *continuous* gray scale, but with all steps of equal width. The value shown in each step is the middle value in the contrast range of the zone it represents. Compared to a continuous scale, a stepped scale is easy to make, hence widely used.

## Tone and Textured Regions of the Gray Scale

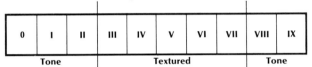

| 0 | I | II | III | IV | V | VI | VII | VIII | IX |
|---|---|----|-----|-----|---|----|-----|------|-----|

Tone     Textured     Tone

**Photographic Scales:** Continuous or stepped, five concern us. In sequence they are: 1) subject value scale, 2) first exposure scale, 3) negative gray scale, 4) second exposure scale, 5) print value scale. All are naturally continuous and each relates in a different way to both the idea of zone and its measurable values.

**Interface:** The time and space between subject values and print values where man and medium meet, technique and sensibilities interact.

**Exposure Zones:** Peculiar to photography, they relate to both meter and negative. When a meter exposure scale is numbered I through IX, each segment is an exposure zone. In photography the luminance of the subject does not determine exposure, but where that reading is placed on the the scale does. Luminance YY is inconsequential until it is placed in exposure zone ZZ.

**Previsualization:** Visualizing the photograph while studying the subject.

**Postvisualization:** When printing a negative remembering back to the plan for the photograph.Or when projecting forward to new combinations.

**Contrast Range:** The maximum lightness and darkness in the entire framed view, negative or print. When measured in stops, it is the number of stops between darkest to lightest: when measured in zones, it *includes* both extremes.

**Local Contrast:** The contrast range found in smaller isolated areas in subjects, negatives and prints.

**Contrast Control:** Exercise of all photographic means to render contrast ranges of subjects and scenes literally or non-literally, as the photographer chooses. Used to exaggerate as well as compensate.

**Place:** To select the value which will determine exposure. Although it can be a Zone V value for any kind of film, with black and white film it is usual to place textured shadow values in Zone III. With Polaroid and color transparencies, as a rule high values are placed.

**Subject Contrast Scales:** They vary widely, sometimes well beyond what light-sensitive materials will handle. Based on optimums, three classes are established—short scale, average scale, and long scale.

**Normal:** Subject contrast scale most suited to the characteristics of the medium that will produce lifelike renderings (9, 10 or 11 zones).

**Expansion:** Increasing contrast in general, by increasing film development time (or decreasing developer dilution, or both) using higher contrast papers, filters, artificial lighting, and so on.

**Compaction:** Decreasing contrast in general by less development time or more dilution, and/or lower paper contrast grades.

**Calibration:** Standardization that connects equipment and materials to photographer, and photographer to the challenge of rendering subject values in print values. The instrument calibrated is the luminance-exposure meter.

**Sensitometry:** Study of the effect of light on silver halides in thin layers. When pictured, appears as curves on graphs.

**Creative:** Anything that might lead us to our Creator.

Certain words commonly used in this system, notably *zone* and *value* have had definition problems. The definitions of these and other words published in the introduction to Ansel Adams' *Pocket Exposure Record* constitute a succinct and well integrated terminology. Dotted with mathematics taken from sensitometry, the whole is elegantly coherent and well fitted to creative photographers who can also think visually in numbers. We warmly recommend it to such photographers.

In this book a few key word definitions seem to be at odds with Adams' terminology. The prime instance is *zone*. In his *Pocket Exposure Record*, (1973; Morgan & Morgan) and in his introduction to the *Zone Systemizer*, Dowdell and Zakia, (1973; Morgan & Morgan) Adams has reduced the scope of the word sharply. Such curtailment is in keeping with his interest in accurate craftsmanship. The present book goes "all out" for zone and zones. We aim to reach creative photographers who at the sight of $c/ft^2$ give up the system.

Zones can be measured in candles per square foot, and what is measured is something that can be seen, it becomes physically present in negative or print. But for visually oriented photographers the zone replaces the numbers. Thinking zonally, we can say "open the shutter speed one zone" or "give it one less zone exposure" and perform the operation with minimum interruption to our flow of visual thinking.

*Value* is another of the words that have both a subjective use and a technical application. As a measurable unit, value has no contrast. (A zone is made up of a small number of values which add up to a very slight range of contrast.) Conceptually the meaning of value overlaps the meaning of zone. For instance when we speak of a Zone V value, we mean any of the values within that zone. So speaking, we refer to the specific single measurement as if it included a cluster of values. Indeed, in many instances of tiny textured subjects that is exactly the case.

Rather than puzzle over which terminology is correct, remember that neither alters the underlying principles, and both have the creative interests of the photographer at heart. The terminologies of the two books are workable variations. Variants of interpretation were forecast and have been encouraged since the beginning of the zone system. The present variations suggest that more personal interpretations within the laws of light-sensitive materials await discovery.

# Visualization by a Zone System

1

**1.** To introduce the previsualization phase of the zone system we can start with almost any photograph. The one at the left will do nicely (1). Notice the distribution of the various values of gray. The values give visibility, their distribution gives shape. While the zone system is mainly concerned with the values, distribution cannot help but affect how we see these values; consequently it is taken into consideration when necessary. For example, black beside white makes both look more intense.

**2**

**2.** By means of visualization, we can mentally redistribute the values of a photograph, reorder them according to some plan. This has been partly attempted with the photograph at the right. (2). It will serve as a sample of possible mental activity. Mentally we could redistribute the values so that all the dark values are gathered at one end and grade into the light values grouped at the other end.

**3.** At (3) we see an idealized sample of arranging all the values of a photograph into a continuous tone scale. We are looking at the range of print values characteristic of the simplest possible form and order, dark to light or light to dark.

**3**

**4**

**4.** If we could slide the scale around on the print (4) it would be obvious to the eye which picture areas match what scale tones. Some kind of connection from the photograph to the abstract tonal values that make it visible could be experienced. In due time a need would make itself felt to talk to oneself about what matched and what didn't. Like inches on a ruler we need some way of identifying parts of the abstract continuous scale. So the continuous value scale is zoned and numbered (5).

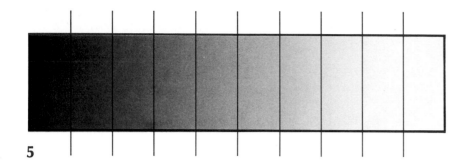

**5.** This zoned continuous scale is memorized for visualization purposes in general, as well as for identifying zones in prints. That is, we convert the actual scale into an *idea* of the scale. However, the remembered scale is rarely identical with its physical and measurable counterpart. Consequently, an imagined or visualized zone and the subjective idea of continuous scale cannot be measured, for they exist only in the mind. But the elastic idea of both scale and zone makes visualization vital and functional, and directly relates to those things which physically exist in the subject, the negative and the print, and which therefore *can* be measured.

**6.** Continuous value gray scales are cumbersome to make and difficult to reproduce faithfully in books. Stepped scales, however, are easier on both counts. With Roman numerals to identify their steps, they are used as stand-ins for the continuous scales. The zone system photographer must remember that each single value in the stepped scale stands near the middle of its respective zone, except for 0 which is all black, and IX which is practically paper white. Either scale works, when held in memory, to identify and visualize subject values in zones. Photographically, the difference from one value to the next on a stepped scale IS EQUAL TO ONE FULL STOP DIFFERENCE IN EXPOSURE. **This is fundamental to understanding and using the zone system!**

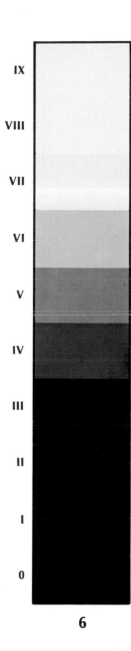

**6**

*The stepped print value scale (6) is always thought of as a stand-in for the zoned continuous value scale (5).*

# Making Zone Rulers

We feel that the reader should make a stepped zone ruler, so zone memorization and seeing can begin at once. Directions are given below for making a zone ruler with Polaroid materials. Later, on page 19, simplified directions are given for using conventional black-and-white materials. Whichever the reader does first is his-her choice.

## A Polaroid Zone Ruler

Polaroid provides the simplest way to make a zone ruler and demonstrate to oneself the method as well as its uses. Polaroid is also a limited contrast control system—a characteristic we take advantage of for the sake of simplicity. Polaroid's in-camera contrast control is limited to exposure. (Out-of-camera contrast controls are available, of course. The primary one in the field is waiting until the incident light changes the subject contrast range; in the studio, we can move fill lights to lighten or darken shadows.)

### Materials and Equipment

1. A Polaroid camera that can let you override its automatic features, or a 4 x 5 view camera with a Polaroid back.

2. An exposure meter. (A camera with through-the-lens metering can be substituted.)

3. Polaroid Film: Type 52, 107, or 105.

4. A white cloth with definite texture (such as a bath towel) as target for all exposures.

5. An 18% neutral gray test card (obtainable at camera stores).

6. A tripod, or other firm camera support.

7. If working indoors, photofloods in reflectors (#1 bulbs).

## Procedure

1. Hang the white cloth in *very even* illumination. Focus on cloth. Cloth image must fill over half of the frame.
2. Set film speed rating in meter. Take a meter reading of cloth only. Expose as meter indicates.
3. The Polaroid print should render the cloth in Zone V, a middle gray. (If the reader is surprised, remember or realize that exposure meters are designed and calibrated to do just that.)
4. Compare print with 18% test card. *Squinting the eyes helps.* (Remember that the gray card represents the middle of Zone V.) If the print is just a *little* lighter or *slightly* darker, consider it to be within Zone V.

   If cloth is rendered *in* Zone V, proceed to the next step.

   If not, any of several variables can be at fault. If the print is *out* of Zone V, adjust exposure in half stops to compensate. Re photograph until the cloth is rendered *in* Zone V. Treat the amount of exposure change required as a factor. * For example if the ASA rating is 400, and one stop more exposure is required to render the cloth in Zone V, then the factor is just one-stop or 200. Apply it to the remaining sheets of film in that box.

*If the print is grossly off,* check the following possible sources of error. Was the proper ASA speed number set into the meter? Did you allow the shadow of your hand or meter to fall on the cloth and distort the meter measurement? Were you careless in setting shutter speed or aperture? Did you correctly follow the sequence of steps related to Polaroid materials? If you have done your part correctly, then perhaps some part of the equipment may need repair or checking. Shutters are the first place to look; they are notoriously unreliable. Another source of error is the light itself. Did the light intensity change from the time the meter was read till the exposure was made? That is a common oversight.

\* The "factor" is a catchall for any number of variables: age and storage conditions of film prior to use, faulty shutter speeds or aperture designations and so on; but not for the photographer's occasional mistakes. To be relieved of remembering the factor at each exposure, the "catchall factor" is set into the meter at the Film Speed Index window.
Please note that the speed of the film has NOT been altered. Never! The film was born with that speed and only old age or improper storage can change it.

*The first print in making a Polaroid zone ruler establishes V to match the 18% neutral gray card.*

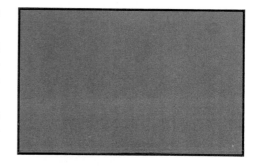

**18% Neutral Test Card**

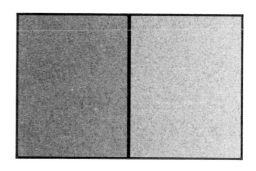

**Approximate limits of Zone V (step)**

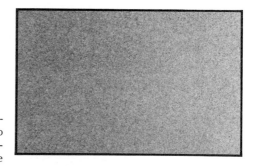

**Approximate limits of Zone V (Continuous)**

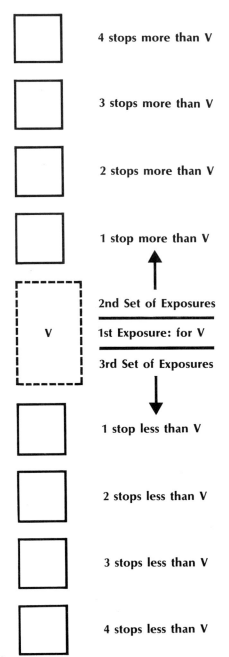

4 stops more than V

3 stops more than V

2 stops more than V

1 stop more than V

↑

2nd Set of Exposures

V    1st Exposure: for V

3rd Set of Exposures

↓

1 stop less than V

2 stops less than V

3 stops less than V

4 stops less than V

When a satisfactory "Zone V cloth" print appears, proceed to the next step. The cloth and the exposure time which produced the Zone V print will be used as the starting point for the next eight photographs.

5. To make the light end of the zone ruler, start with an exposure *one stop more* than that given the Zone V print above. Progressively make four prints, giving each one stop more exposure than the preceding print.

6. To make the dark end of the scale, start with an exposure *one stop less* than the Zone V exposure. Make four prints, each at one stop less exposure than the preceding print.

The fourth exposure at each end of the zone ruler may be one too many. When we have had no experience with Polaroid, the extra exposures allow us to discriminate more precisely which is the first solid black (after the darkest gray), and which print is the first maximum bright. (Incidentally, notice that the maximum bright in a Polaroid image is never as white as the border.)

7. Cut off one white border of each of the nine prints. Overlap them and mount so that the prints (Zones) progress from dark to light without a white line between to disturb vision. Customarily the darkest is at the left end of the scale, the brightest at the right. The prints may be mounted so as to fold up consecutively. Then the zone ruler fits into a pocket.

Notice that the new zone ruler is a discontinuous gray scale. It is also called a step-scale. When using the stepped scale, we repeat, remember that each value *represents* the middle of its zone.

**The Exposure Series for the Polaroid Zone Ruler**
*No reasons exist that would forbid reversing the order of the 2nd and 3rd exposure sequences.*

## Things to Observe About the Polaroid Zone Ruler

To locate the three tone and texture regions of the new scale, identify the prints (Zones) which show the texture of the cloth, and those which do not. We can expect to find cloth texture present in the middle zones and missing from prints at either end. Only tones (or *values*) are present at the ends of the scale, but these are valuable to maintain a sense of contrast in photographs. The two lightest prints are likely to show almost the same shade of gray, and are probably textureless. And neither of them is as white as the border; this is typical of Polaroid materials.

To find the contrast scale of the Polaroid material, we count the number of textured zones (prints) *between* darkest and lightest, then add two (for the darkest and lightest). If, for example, six textured prints appear, we assume the material has an 8-zone capacity or range. From the standpoint of overall scale we can say this another way. The contrast range of any black-and-white material is always black through white. That range is fairly consistent. The difference among paper grades is the number of segments available *between* black and white. The short scale papers have fewer segments or zones, the long scale papers have more. Type 52 Polaroid materials have a total of only about seven zones. As we begin to realize these differences, we begin to understand that the zone is an elastic unit. We will see later that Zone III in Polaroid is darker than Zone III in conventional materials. Visual photographers have been heard to say, "Polaroid never gets to Zone IX white, and drops to Zone I black fast."

## First Practical Application for the Polaroid Zone Ruler

After making a Polaroid contrast scale, we can use the exposure meter to indicate when the contrast range is too much for that Polaroid material, when too little, and when right on.

We could call this, "Using the Luminance Meter to Tell When Not to Expose Polaroid." Instead it is really about what to expect when we expose Polaroid to each of the three main classes of subject contrast ranges: too little, too much, or right on. Thus the choice, to expose or not to expose, is left up to the photographer. Speaking negatively, if the subject contrast range is too long for the Polaroid 7-zone scale (3), or too short for it (2), don't shoot. If the two ranges are about equal (1), yes!

## Three Classes of Subject Contrast and the Polaroid Response

**1. When the subject contrast range and the Polaroid scale match**

| | | V | Subject |
|---|---|---|---|

| | | V | Film |
|---|---|---|---|

17

When the subject contrast range is less **than four** zones on the luminance meter, the rule of thumb is, find another picture. On the positive side, mitigating circumstances and expressive considerations can turn any rule of thumb upside-down. For example, the photographer likes flat prints, and especially the subject at hand so rendered, (2). Speaking negatively again, if the contrast range exceeds eight zones (3), again the mental indicator goes red: stop, don't shoot. But if one wants black silhouettes, the eye's green light goes on—so expose. Frequently, contrasty renderings are as psychologically revealing or as aesthetically stimulating as low contrast images, for entirely different reasons, of course.

If the reader has made a zone ruler for Polaroid, he will be ready to consider exposure-control options, page 43.

**2. When subject contrast is less than Polaroid scale**

| | V | Subject |
|---|---|---|

| | V | Film |
|---|---|---|

**3. When subject contrast is greater than Polaroid scale.**

| | V | Subject |
|---|---|---|

| | V | Film |
|---|---|---|

*Expose Polaroid frequently to the "too long" and "too short" ranges. Anticipate finding ways to produce vital images even though the contrast situation is anything but optimum. Reflectors, "fill-in" flash, waiting till the light changes, and filters all help, when used correctly, to lessen contrast or increase contrast as required.*

## A Conventional B&W Zone Ruler

Assuming that the reader exposes, develops and prints his or her own negatives, a B&W zone ruler should be simple to make. To avoid complexities at this moment, we ask that you use your customary methods without alteration for the occasion. As in making the Polaroid zone scale, the only variable will be exposure. The result may be barely tolerable as compared to the adjusted zone ruler to be made later during Calibration, but for visualization purposes over-precision is not a prime requisite. (In fact beginning students of zone system photography generally fall into the trap of exactness beyond the tolerances of aperture and shutter speed variations.)

### Preparation: Similar to Making Polaroid Zone Scale
White cloth as target.
Film   Roll: 2 rolls. Sheet: 15 sheets.
Luminance meter. (Any meter that you know how to use.)
18% neutral test card.
Medium contrast grade printing paper.
Lighting Outdoors: either overcast, or sun slightly to one side.
Lighting Studio: two lights at 45° angles, one on each side. One about half the distance from towel as the other, to increase texture slightly.
Patience.

### Production
1. The first step is to reach a standard-print-exposure-time.
   A. Determine a Zone V exposure for towel from meter. Expose one frame (or sheet) as indicated.
   B. Expose 3 frames (3 sheets) progressively 1/2 stop *less* than indicated.
   C. Expose 3 frames (3 sheets) progressively 1/2 stop *more than indicated.*
   D. *Develop first roll (or first six sheets) according to your customary procedure.*
   E. When dry take any one of the negatives and print the blank, we repeat, BLANK, clear edge to find the shortest exposure that makes it maximum black. For this step the sprocket

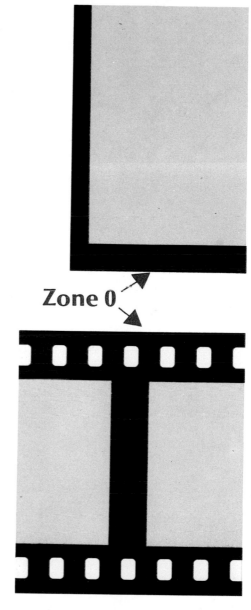

Zone 0

*The **minimum** exposure required to print the blank edges Zone 0 is taken as standard-print-exposure time.*

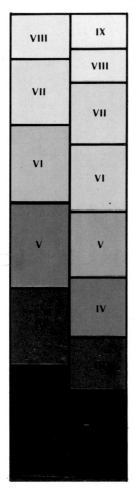

Polaroid    Conventional

## Comparison of Polaroid and Conventional zone rulers

*When we generate both rulers from Zone V, we definitely see that the Zone III in Polaroid is darker than the Zone III in conventional B&W. For visualization this means that we have to adjust our mental* **idea** *of, say, Zone III, according to our experience of the film in the camera. Note also how Polaroid differs from conventional in the zones above V.*

holes in 35mm film are a great boon. When the image of the film base around the holes almost matches (it never quite matches exactly) the black of the holes, that exposure is taken as standard-print-exposure-time. (Use a medium paper grade exclusively for the zone ruler.) Not only is the edge to be maximum black, but it must be achieved by the *minimum exposure time.*

2. The second step is to find which Zone V exposure comes the closest to matching the 18% test card.
   A. Apply the new standard-print-exposure-time *without further adjustment* to the remainder of the negatives.
   B. Whichever print, when dry, comes the closest to matching the 18% gray card is assigned Zone V status. Some of the others may also be within Zone V, but we are seeking the middle value of the zone.
   C. Make a note of the camera exposure time of that negative. This is the adjusted Zone V exposure; use it as the starting point for the remainder of the steps.
3. The third step is to expose the zone ruler.* Expose the second roll of film (or sheets) to the cloth target.
   A. To make the lighter steps of the scale, expose four sheets (or frames) each progressively one stop more than the adjusted Zone V exposure. This will produce Zones VI, VII, VIII, and IX.
   B. To make the darker steps of the scale, expose four sheets each progressively one stop less than the adjusted Zone V exposure. This will produce Zones IV, III, II, and I.
4. Complete the zone ruler.
   A. Print each negative at *exactly* the same time as the standard-print-exposure-time. If using an enlarger, the f-stop and lens-to-print distance must be *exactly* the same as before.

---

* Before starting to actually make a zone ruler, write out an exposure schedule consistent with the shutter speeds and apertures of your equipment. See page 53 in Calibrations.
  A further restriction must be recognized: Keep exposures to one second or less. This is to avoid an adverse reciprocity effect that yields less exposure than planned. See Appendix C.

**B.** When the prints are dry, trim off the white edges and mount squares of one-inch or so in the customary order: black to the left, white to the right. Compare it to the zone ruler printed on the back of this book.

The result should be ten steps, eight of which are different shades of gray between solid black and unshaded white. The middle five zones will show texture, the rest little or no texture; no print will be identical with another—close but not identical. The reader may find that his zone ruler does not quite fit this ideal. If so, let it stand for now. Probably the reason will be found in the film development time, too short or too long. Even though the ruler is primarily a clear picture of how your processing procedures work, you can use the present ruler for an introduction to previsualization. Later, during the calibration runs, a zone ruler will be produced that will fit the definition of Normal by development time as well as exposure time.

| Polaroid | 0 | II | III | IV | V | VI | VII | VIII |
|---|---|---|---|---|---|---|---|---|
| Conventional | 0 | I | II | III | IV | V | VI | VII | VIII | IX |

**Comparison of Polaroid and Conventional scales by width of steps**

*The idea of zone is elastic. Because the idea is not fixed, it serves the practice of visualization well. The stepped print scale (Polaroid or B&W) shows only one value per zone. Consequently that one value represents the whole area of the zone. As the bullseye on a target has diameter, the zone has dimension. The area of the zone amounts to a tolerance comparable to the variations acceptable in shutter speeds and apertures.*

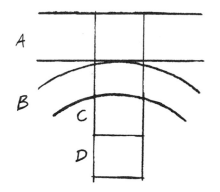

A

B

C

D

## Coupling Zone Rulers to Luminance Meters

The moment has arrived to elucidate the coupling of print zone rulers to the exposure scale of exposure meters.

Because of the numerous luminance meter types in use, we need a symbol for visualization. In the adjacent diagram, (A) represents the zone ruler and print exposure scale; (B) the meter's light value scale; (C) the aperture; and (D) the shutter speed. This form of the symbol originates out of the Weston exposure meters; but with some imagination may be applied mentally to connecting zone ruler to light measurements.

Coupling of zone ruler to meter is generally done by rotating dials so that some one zone of/the ruler (A in the symbols) is opposite some one particular light value reading (B in the symbol). For example in the figure below, a 7 light value reading is shown opposite Zone V. With an ASA of 100, an aperture of f/8 requires a 4 second exposure.

Once coupled by *placement*, here light value 7 was placed opposite Zone V, the meter then indicates in what zones the other light value readings will *fall*. In the figure below, light reading 5 falls in Zone III and light value 10 falls in Zone VIII. Let's take another example: if light value reading 7 were placed in (opposite) Zone VIII, the aperture of f/16 would indicate 120 seconds exposure.

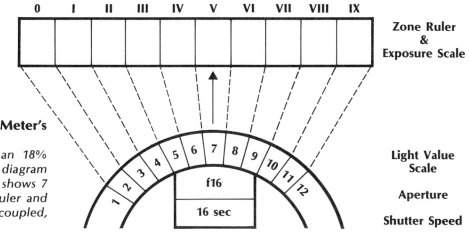

### Print Zone Ruler Coupled to Meter's Exposure Scale

*The illustrations assume that an 18% gray card read light value 7. The diagram shows 7 opposite V. That is, it shows 7 placed in V. Now print zone ruler and exposure scale of the meter are coupled, connected, superimposed.*

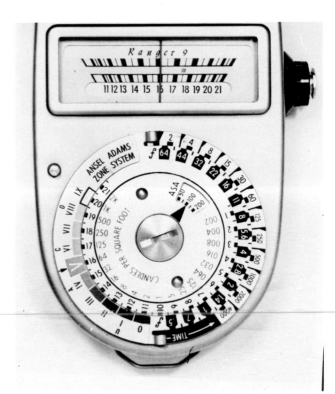

The same subject was metered at dawn and again at noon. The meters above show the difference. Zone V was placed in each instance. The symbols below show the same information.

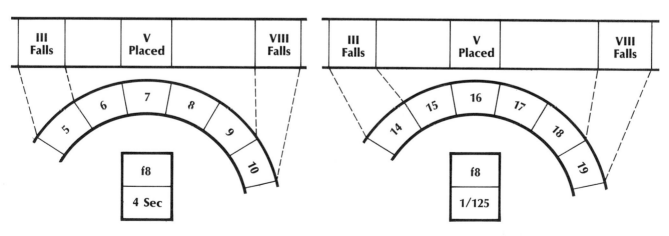

**Subject measured at dawn**

**Same subject measured at noon**

## Reading Meters in Zones.

**Few meters have space for zone rulers; so they are read by stops.**

*Because exposure meters average for Zone V (or VI), to find an exposure for Zone III Placement from a closeup meter reading, give two stops less exposure. Count down three zones; for example f/8 at 1/25; f/8 at 1/50; and f/8 at 1/100= Zone III exposure for an f/8 1/25 shadow reading.*

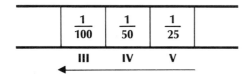

**Count down 3 stops from indicated exposure to find exposure for Zone III.**

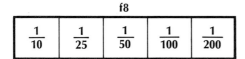

**A 5-zone Contrast**

Luminance meters, both in and out of cameras, come in such a wide assortment that we aim to point out the essentials which make them readable in zones.

**1.** Luminance meters average the light intensities reaching their light-sensitive cells. Even the 1- and 2-degree spot meters average, though the smallness of the angle overcomes the effect. Consequently unless one takes account of the contrast or range of tones present within the meter's view, errors are bound to happen. Prevent metering mistakes by moving in so close that the contrast of the area measured is within one zone. To be sure, that is not always possible. When moving in with 7- to 30-degree averaging meters, watch closely that meter, hand or body does not interfere with the light falling on the subject. The danger is real.

**2.** Meters that do not guide exposure with "stop" and "go" lights, indicate exposures in apertures, shutter speeds, and stops. To use these data for readings in zones, remember that most luminance meters are manufactured so that any single reading indicates a Zone V exposure! A few indicate Zone VI. Do not take anyone's word for this. Take meter readings of three textureless, monotoned walls, one dark, one light and one middle gray. Expose according to the meter's indications, develop all three identically. Except for gross errors, all three negatives, or Polaroid prints, will be in Zone V, or sometimes Zone VI.

**3.** *Counting Stops* To read in zones the *subject contrast range*, meter the low value (shadow) and note exposure, e.g. (f/4 at 1/25 sec). Then read the brights and again note the exposure indicated (f/16 at 1/25 sec). Count the number of F/stops (f/4, 5.6, 8, 11, 16 =5 stops). The number of stops equals the number of zones (5 zones in the example given*).

**4.** *Contrast-Control Indications* To read in zones the *control* of subject contrast, four basic assumptions are made. (They are often revised to fit particular picture taking situations.)

    A.  The low reading will be placed in Zone III.

    B.  The high values will be "brought to" Zone VII by variable

* Sensitometrists do this differently: they count the number of stops *between* lowest and highest. So a 5 zone contrast range to the Zone systemized photographer is thought of as a 4 stop contrast range by the sensitometrist.

film development, various paper contrast grades, lighting, filters, or combinations thereof.

C. When controls are exercised, the result will be a standard, full-scale print of 9, 10, or 11 zones. (Called Normal)

D. Shadow values placed in textured Zone III will usually include Zones 0, I, and II. (When included, even though automatically, it helps produce the sensation of texture in Zone III.)

High values "brought to" textured Zone VII by exercise of contrast-controls will frequently include Zones VIII and IX, especially if "averaging" light meters are used. (These zones help produce the sense of texture in Zone VII.)

Obviously these assumptions are violated more often than kept.

5. The table below will consolidate the assumptions above.

| Subject Zones | Contrast Range | Control* Symbol | Print Zones Predicted |
|---|---|---|---|
| III-V | 3 zones | N+2 | 0-IX |
| III-VI | 4 zones | N+1 | 0-IX |
| III-VII | 5 zones | N | 0-IX |
| III-VIII | 6 zones | N-1 | 0-IX |
| III-IX | 7 zones | N-2 | 0-IX |

## Moving Needle/Fixed Pointer Meters

In meters of the moving needle and fixed pointer type, when needle and pointer line up, the indicated exposure is Zone V. Any other markings on either side of the pointer usually represent changes in full stops. Hence they can be read as equivalent zones higher or lower than Zone V. Through-the-lens meters usually omit such markings. In such cases it is easy to visually estimate the zones over and under V. Sight through the eyepiece, line up needle and pointer, then change shutter speed (or aperture) one stop. Mentally note the distance the needle moves to the right or left of the pointer. With practice one can quickly learn to judge as much as two zones on either side of Zone V. (The circle on the needle of the Canon F-1 is just one zone wide.)

\* N+ and N− are symbols for altered development time of the film, and/or printing on a higher or lower, respectively, contrast grade of paper than that used for Normal. For example N+1 means developing the film longer, "one zone's worth," so that an area exposed for Zone VII will have the density in the negative of Zone VIII. This is called "expansion." "Compaction" means just the opposite: less development and/or a lower contrast grade of paper.

## Reading meters by stops, continued

*Because exposure meters average for V (or VI) to make a placement of a bright reading in Zone VII, for example, count up 3 stops from the indicated exposure.*

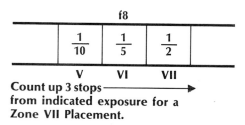

| | f8 | | | |
|---|---|---|---|---|
| | $\frac{1}{10}$ | $\frac{1}{5}$ | $\frac{1}{2}$ | |
| | V | VI | VII | |

**Count up 3 stops from indicated exposure for a Zone VII Placement.**

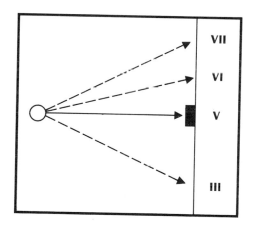

**Symbol of Through-the-Lens Exposure Meters**

*By moving the whole camera in close with in-camera meters, they can be used to measure the light reflected from small areas just as hand held meters can.*

## Exercises in Visualization

When we understand how the zone ruler is connected to the meter dials, we can start to visualize with it.

1. Look at some white cloth and decide which of all the possible tonal renderings is the most literal. Most of us would identify or associate the textured cloth with Zone VIII or thereabouts. Having made the decision, how do we produce the photograph we want? There is more than one way of doing that, but for the sake of oversimplification just now we will note only two. (In the following examples we assume an ASA of 100 and a light value of 9 opposite Zone V). Knowing that Zone VIII is three stops above Zone V, we would plan three stops more exposure than the meter indicated for Zone V (f/4 at 1/25). (The reader already has this picture on his zone ruler.) Twice the exposure produced the Zone VI cloth picture; four times, the Zone VII photograph; and eight times, the Zone VIII rendering (f/4 at 1/4 second).

A more direct manipulation to arrive at the same result (cloth in Zone VIII) is to rotate the meter dial so that light value 9 is opposite Zone VIII on the zone ruler. The indicated exposure is f/4 at 1/4 second. This method is typical zone system practice.

2. With eyes closed, visualize a Zone III rendering of cloth. Open eyes and check the Zone III gray on the zone ruler; and then use the meter to compute a Zone III exposure. Try the same with other zonal options.

3. Visualize any other zone renderings *while looking at the cloth, eyes open.* Try to estimate indicated exposure. Then use the meter to check your estimate. Are any of the options more interesting than the literal one?

The reader will find that visualizing photographs approximately as eyes see subjects, offers no particular problems. But visualizing the whole subject or various parts of it as lighter or darker than the eye identifies them is more difficult. One may not be able to hallucinate the visualized tonality. But with the help of the zone ruler one can learn to "sense" subject values in zones different than the eye reports. Opportunities to use it abound. Almost every potential photograph has some areas that film and paper will render darker than the eye sees them.

*In certain meters such as Pentax 1/21, a more direct way to reach an indicated exposure is to move the dials so that the critical area determines the exposure. For example the towel was needed in Zone VIII, so its light reading of 9 was "swung" opposite VIII. The resulting exposure will produce the desired rendering.*

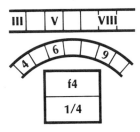

*In the case of a normal scene, whether one places the shadow value, the high value, or the Zone V value, will not change the indicated exposure.*

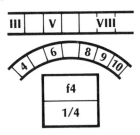

# I Want

From the experience of the above exercise in visualization a fundamental question emerges, "What do I want my photograph to look like?"

It is not too early to bring up this question because many students will expect this book to tell them what kind of photographs to want. The zone system can help the photographer achieve what *he* wants in pictures (within the limits of the medium), but must never be relied upon to set standards. The inevitable standards such as the Normal print, are to be taken as starting points for exploration of all the options, not dogma.

"What zone values do I want to render the cloth in?" That is the question! The essence of that question underlies all photography whether the photographer knows how to get it into the print or doesn't. The snapshooter is satisfied with anything the camera gives; the professional only with what he or she can make it yield. In between stands the student who thinks he is "supposed" to want something, and wonders what.

In almost any photographic situation the literal or near-literal is not the only option. Though it may be the only kind of rendering that the photographer wants, the literal may also be exactly what he-she wants to avoid. The zone ruler based on the textured cloth shows the options of a special instance: the subject is monotone and the changes are held to exposure alone. Nevertheless, the reader's ruler is evidence of several optional renderings, most of them non-literal. To have so many options is exceptional; in most photographs the choices are limited.

Newcomers to the system have a great time at first deciding in what zone they want this and that. Such a cavalier freedom with the system stimulates a marvelous sense of free play until the medium asserts itself and refuses to comply.

One firm feature of photography is the persistence of the tonal sequences found in the original subject. A Zone III next to a Zone V in the original retains the same dark-to-light relation in the print, though not necessarily the same three-zone separation. If two more zones (or stops) exposures were given, the three-zone separation would be seen as Zones V and VIII.

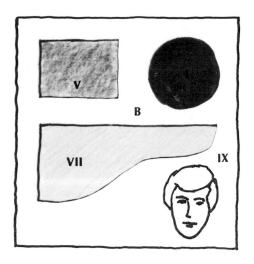

**The Dilemma of Tonal Sequence**

*The sketch represents three areas of a subject. The numbers represent metered zones based on matching Zone V in subject. The photographer looking at the subject decides what he wants and then looks at the meter to see if that is possible.*

*I want the square in Zone III, ☐ the circle in Zone V, ☐ and the other one in IX ☐ . Can I have it?*

*The meter says, "No, the square will be middle gray, the circle dark and the other one light."*

*Tonal sequences generally retain their original <u>order</u> even though contrast differences may be altered between various areas. Strong filters can alter tonal sequences in some instances.*

Polaroid Type 52

| III |
|-----|

| 14 |
|----|

| f45 |
|-----|
| 1/60 |

**Simple Beginnings of Visualizing Entire Photographs.**
**1.** Find a multi-zoned subject contrast range of seven to eight zones.
**2.** Expose and process as if making a 10-zone ruler.
**3.** Adjust first exposure so Zone V matches 18% test card.
**4.** Make succeeding exposures in one-stop changes.
**5.** Mount as in model below.

Reading at 14
taken from
middle panel

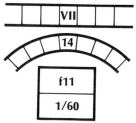

The reproductions on the previous pages satisfactorily present the *idea* of previsualizing whole scenes at once, but not the experience. The reader needs to make his own series for that. Operationally the series is akin to a zone ruler. In each successive exposure the light value reading of the key area is *placed* one zone higher or lower. In zone system thinking, this succession is not just a matter of giving one stop more or less exposure each time. It is that, to be sure, but the zone system photographer adds a dimension to the operation. He *places* the critical area of his attention *in whatever zone he wants* and exposes accordingly. Then studies the results for future visualization data.

The quantity of information to be unearthed in this "field zone-ruler" is extensive, and some of it too subtle for book reproduction to convey. So we say again that the reader should simulate the series with a subject of his-her own choosing. When the series is mounted, try to observe how contrasts change in each picture from one end of the series to the other. This is grist for future previsualization. Notice how the middle values respond to one- or two-zone changes as compared to what happens at either end. Try to observe the mental acrobatics that occur during the process of visualizing an entire planned photograph one zone darker or lighter than the eye claims. Then try two zones, and so on.

## Ten Fingers Ten Zones

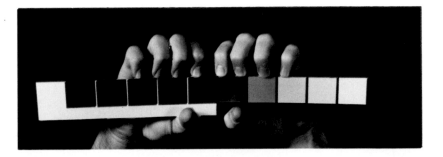

# Zonal Identifications of Subject Tonalities

When we extend the idea of zone to subject matter, we enter a subjective realm indeed. We each impose on the view some idiosyncratic idea of it. Trying to record the visual world "out there" into a scale from darkest to lightest, as we did a photograph at the beginning of this section, poses problems that are primarily semantic. Scientists study the psychophysical connections between subject values and print values; but who will doubt the presence of a visual connection? In order to avoid shooting unphotographically, like robots, we need some connection between subject and print that incorporates the photometric. In other words, to be significantly different from ordinary seeing, seeing photographically, requires that some kind of visual connection be made between values in the subject and values in the final print. In this system, of course the concept is the "zone". And the means is imagination to make the thought of "zone" into the necessary bridge. The elastic idea of "zone" is the prime means of visually correlating subject tonalities with print tonalities (when backed up with the physical and measurable "zone").

Early in the development of a zone system, Adams and Archer prepared a table of Zone and Subject Correlates that still stands as a workable guideline whenever the photographer prefers lifelike renderings. Their table of subject tonalities in zones is nothing more nor less than a print gray scale applied to subject matter. Arbitrary, literal, and approximate as it is, the imagination finds their table viable during previsualization, both as a standard for the lively literal and, as pointed out earlier, as a starting point for the expressive non-literal.

The perennial problem in making use of a subject value scale originates at times in psychological quirks, and at other times in physiological characteristics. Psychologically we keep imposing our *idea* of a thing on it whenever we see that thing. This guarantees our not seeing any thing as it is, and especially not as photography records it. Our *idea* of black, for instance, is colored by our experiences and associations: funerals, sexy dresses, racial differences, and so on. And, of course, no two persons have the same set of associations. Films and lenses, by the way, have no *idea* of black, or gray or white.

*When we hold a calibrated and zoned meter up to a subject and take readings, we are enabled to visualize (imagine) the view **as if** its subject values were print values. For example, to our surprise, we learn that in a scene where middle greys in the subject match corresponding areas in the prints, the print black and white do not match subject blacks and whites! By such a use of meter and ruler we introduce some objectivity into our ordinarily un-photographic seeing.*

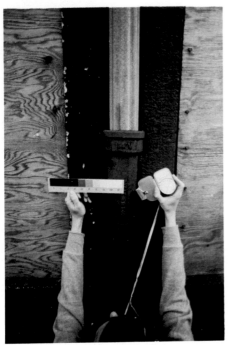

**Subject Values Correlated to Print Zones**

Physiologically the eye plays some tricks on vision. A familiar example is called "simultaneous contrast". A square of middle gray surrounded by a large square of black appears decidedly lighter than the same gray square in a white surrounding. The luminance meter, if read with awareness and understanding, can help us visualize the gray square "as it is", and as photography will "see it". (Another example occurs when Zone II dark is found next to Zone VIII light; the effect on the eye is as if the zones were 0 and IX. So one can imagine the added sense of contrast or brilliance when IX and 0 are adjacent.) Reading luminance meters with awareness leads us to realize both the psychological and physiological factors that prevent us from seeing photographically.

Neuropsychologist Richard L. Gregory, in his book *Intelligent Eye* describes some of the adjustments our eyes make to size and brightness that the camera does not see. Psychologists refer to such adjustments as *Adaptation*.

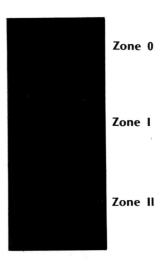

Photo paper black; maximum black representing emptiness; nothing; openings into unlit rooms. Seems solid, rather than mysterious.

Zone 0

Nearly black, the beginnings of a sense of empty space. Unlit rooms; forests; depths; shadows in dim light.

Zone I

The first sense of an emergence of texture. On the border line between visible and invisible texture—mysterious.

Zone II

TEXTURED SHADOW. Texture and detail are firm and full of the sense of substance in dark materials such as black garments, leather. Visible creases and folds encourage the sense of touch.

Average dark foliage, dark stone, shadow in landscape or buildings. Recommended shadow zone for portraits in sunlight or floodlight.

The pivotal zone for both paper and film. Middle gray; 18% neutral test card. Dark or sunburned skin in sunlight; clear North sky on panchromatic film; average weathered wood or stone; light foliage.

Caucasian skin with sunlight, but not glare or highlights. Snow in shadow when both sun and shadow are in the same picture. Clear North sky with orthochromatic film. Poured concrete buildings in overcast light.

TEXTURED BRIGHTS. Light skin entirely in diffuse light. Average snow in raking sun; light gray concrete; bright colors. "Whites" with textures and delicate values. Sense of substance remains tactile.

Last vestiges of texture. Glaring surfaces; snow in flat light; whites without texture.

Threshold gray into pure white of the paper. Tends to feel solid representing only itself. Loss of sense of substance. Represents highlights (as opposed to brights) such as chrome trim, or specular reflections.

This table is useful when starting to visualize. It will help to prime the pump. If we don't consider it as dogma now, later when we have outgrown it, we will look back with kind memories.

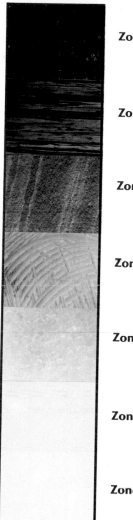

Zone III

Zone IV

Zone V

Zone VI

Zone VII

Zone VIII

Zone IX

# Photographing by a Zone System: General Outline of Steps

This outline will acquaint the reader with a simplified basic routine of making photographs by the zone system before he or she has taken the opportunity to calibrate equipment and material. An exercise follows the outline; by doing it the reader may put the system to work in a few hours—tentatively to be sure.

## Steps in a Two-Reading Routine

1. *Choose subject, or let subject choose you.*
2. *Meter-read shadows—low*
3. *"       " brights—high*
4. *Count subject contrast range in zones*
5. *First sampling of possibilities:* **place** *shadow reading in Zone III, observe where high reading* **falls.** *If in Zone VIII or higher, compactions are indicated; if in VI or below, expansions are indicated (to produce Normal prints)*
*6. *Calculate and previsualize other options as well as the full-scale one*
*7. *Decide on one option and write out its plan for production (f/stop, shutter speed, film development, and paper grade)*
8. *Expose, process film and print as planned*
9. *Study final print for fulfillment of plan*
10. *In preparation for the next photograph, critique plan for fulfillment of intention, or fulfillment of "I want"*

The above routine is elaborated and refined in the Calibration Section.

## Preparation

1. Conventional B&W film, roll or sheet; whatever brand and type you regularly use.
2. Know how to read your luminance meter in zones (general information in section on meters).
3. Familiar brand and grades of photographic paper.
4. Whatever processing skills you already have.
5. Attentive reading of instructions (photographers in general are notorious for having a hard time with printed words).

The outline steps include both the *exposure* that affects overall darkness and lightness of the photograph, and the *contrast-control* that deals with the compensation for subject contrast ranges other than those best suited to the medium. To keep the outline cut to the bone, contrast-control symbols are used: Normal (N), Normal Plus (N+), and Normal Minus (N−). The symbols stand for variable film development (time/dilution), various paper contrast grades, and contrast control by combinations of film development and paper grades.

Just as the exposure control of the image is previsualized, so are the effects of subject contrast control. Exercises for the latter appear in the Calibration section because the topic is too complex to deal with before the calibrations are done.

The meter reading method presented in the outline has been called the "two-tone Zone System". It is the simplest of several sophisticated ways applicable to planning photographs in zones.

*Creative action in this routine peaks in and near Steps 6 and 7. (Interface)

**1.** Select a scene or subject

To begin with, make meter reading easy for yourself. Find a subject with fairly large, broadly-textured low contrast areas. Illustration (A) is an example of a subject that can be measured more or less correctly by anyone just starting to read exposure meters in zones. Experience will provide the data to read with assurance such high contrast and finely textured subjects as bushes or trees in full leaf (B).

**2.** Move luminance meter in close to dark areas but not so close that hand and meter cast a shadow

Measure shadow areas. This is taken to mean the *darkest area to be rendered with texture.*
(For example the meter reading is 6.)

**3.** Move meter in close to bright areas but not so close that hand and meter intercept any light falling on subject

Measure light-valued areas. This is taken to mean the lightest areas in which *texture is expected.* (It does *not* include specular reflections or highlights. These are usually too small to read accurately. They also record best without texture. Speculars are pre-visualized as tiny "white keys".)
(For example, the meter reading is 10.)

A

*Learn to meter on large simple areas*

*When metering, move in close, very close*

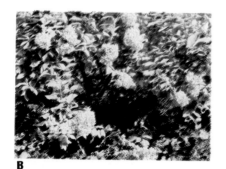

B

*Learn to read subjects with complex textures and small areas by substitution.*

*Find areas near by that are large and have the same reflectances, they can be read accurately.*

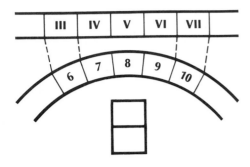

**A 5-zone subject**

**4.** First sampling of subject contrast

The aim is a preliminary sampling of the subject contrast range in units of zones. It will be used in working out a final contrast-control decision. The range is counted from the meter's light value numbers. In the example at hand—light value numbers 6 (low) and 10 (high)—there are five numbers: 6, 7, 8, 9, 10, and so five zones. (When we count contrast range in *stops,* the difference is one less than the total number of zones. The present example has a five-*zone* contrast range, but a four-*stop* contrast range.)

In the two-reading method, promptly determining the subject contrast range establishes a quick clue to what class of contrast-control is likely to be required. The range of five textured zones is taken as the full-scale standard (Normal). This is seen in the present example. Fewer than five textured zones is classed as short-scale and more than five is classed as long-scale.

Note that the five zones are *textured* zones. In the sketchy two-reading method, we take for granted that untextured zones are included automatically, some darker than textured shadow, and some lighter than textured bright.

**5.** Exposure by placement in Zone III

Textured shadow is defined as the darkest part of the subject in which detail is "wanted". Whatever dark texture is rendered in Zone III will be visible as texture; Zone II and lower will be without texture. So exposure is set by placement of textured shadow in Zone III. (This implies that areas may be present in the subject darker than III with textures that are allowed to disappear in the darkness of Zones I and II in the print.)

If your personal exposure meter "averages" at Zone V, it will be easy to understand why giving a shadow reading two stops less exposure than indicated "places" textured shadow in Zone III. Zone III is two stops less than Zone V.

Zone system users produce the same placement and exposure in a slightly different way. They rotate meter dials so that the textured shadow reading is opposite the Zone III of the implied Zone Ruler on the meter dials.

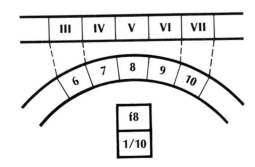

**A Zone III placement to set exposure**

**6.** Contrast control indicated by fall of textured bright

After an exposure control setting or placement of textured *shadow* in Zone III, contrast control is indicated by where the textured *bright* falls. If it falls opposite Zone VII on the meter's implied zone ruler, Normal contrast control is suggested.

If the high reading falls in Zone VI or below, Normal Plus control is required to compensate. When only one zone compensations are desired, the photographer has a choice: either a Plus 1 negative, or a higher grade of paper.

If the high reading falls in Zone VIII or above, the opposite holds: Normal Minus control is suggested to compensate for too long a subject contrast range.

As we see in the table below, the long- and short-scale subject contrast ranges are identified in units of zones. So are the options Normal Minus and Normal Plus. When N stands for Normal, N−1 stands for Normal Minus one zone; N+1 stands for Normal Plus one zone, and so on up to options N−3 and N+3. Beyond that is theoretical.

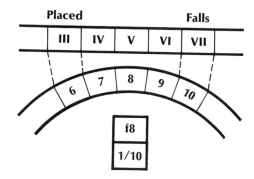

*Light reading 10 falls in Zone VII. This indicates Normal contrast control.*

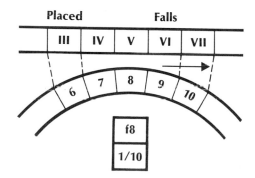

*Low in III, high reading falls in Zone VI. Indicates Normal-plus-1 contrast control so that that VI area will print as if it had been VII.*

### Contrast-Control in Zones*

(Based on the five textured zones)

| Subject Contrast Range | | | Contrast Control Symbol | | |
|---|---|---|---|---|---|
| | 9 | zone range | N −4 | | (Compactions) |
| Long- | 8 | " " | N −3 | | |
| Scaled | 7 | " " | N −2 | | |
| | 6 | " " | N −1 | Normal Minus Options | |
| Normal | 5 | " " | N | Normal Option | |
| | 4 | " " | N +1 | Normal Plus Options | |
| Short- | 3 | " " | N +2 | | |
| Scaled | 2 | " " | N +3 | | (Expansions) |
| | 1 | " " | N +4 | | |

*This five-*textured*-zone scale is most useful in the two-reading method under discussion. Because of its simplicity it should be of interest to roll film photographers. But it is not the only scale. During calibrations, other scales especially applicable to large format photography and "fine tuning" will be introduced.

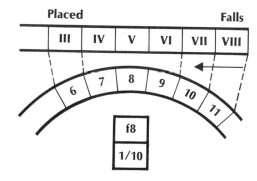

*Low in III, high reading falls in Zone VIII. This indicates Normal-minus-1 contrast control.*

Two other considerations are included in this sixth step. (1) Sometimes a near-literal rendering will be more truthful to the *feeling* of the original subject than a value-for-value literal picture. So small changes are willingly made for the purpose of being faithful to the spirit as well as the letter of the original. (2) When the subject contrast range is in the neighborhood of two or more zones over or under the five textured zones, compromises and sacrifices are expected in order to produce the lifelike Normal photograph. That is, some mental calculations and visual manipulations must be exercised.

**7.** Previsualize possibilities and options other than normal

Thus far in the outline, the work with meter and zone ruler relates only to the option of the full-scale Normal photograph because normal is what the meter is calibrated to. When in the sixth step the Normal picture possibility has appeared in our mind's eye, we begin in the seventh to visualize the effect of exposure controls and contrast controls singly or combined. (While the reader is not yet prepared to visualize contrast controls, he-she will soon learn.) When we investigate what kind of non-literal renderings are open to the photographer, seven fairly distinct categories appear in a continuous scale of possibilities (three on either side of Normal).

> Overscaled: dark, middle, light
> Normal
> Underscaled: low key, middle key, high key

When these options are produced by exposure changes alone, they are not as dramatic as when combined with the Plus or Minus contrast controls and special films and developers commonly used expressively.

Zone system photographers use meters calibrated to Normal rendering; consequently Normal becomes the starting point for any exploration they choose to make of dramatization, investigations of the strange and the marvelous, and even the symbolism of tonal values: black for the depths of man, grays for the mundane and misty, white for the heights of experience, and all the rest of this arcane topic.

*Creative activity peaks at Steps 6 and 7 according to this outline. At this time photographers are using the meter to reveal various picture possibilities of the subject, so far as tonalities go. They are actively putting their imagination to the task of previsualizing the possibilities.*
*In Step 7 they exercise the creative aspect of choice among possibilities. They may decide to photograph only one, or to postpone any decision and photograph them all.*

*During this period they can get lost in the mechanics of the decisions. But they can also use choice-making as a way of making contact with any "meaning" of the subject and sustaining resonance with it.*

The various natures of the subjects themselves affect the options. Some subjects offer numerous possibilities and several options; others are quite restrictive and present one or no options. Whichever, few or several, must be determined on the spot for each potential photograph. When some, if not all, of the possibilities presented by the subject and screened by the medium have been visualized, exercise the option of your choice, select one (or more) and render photographically.

**8.** Write out plans for the chosen option

Once decided upon, the plan is simple: record exposure control and contrast control. The first is recorded as f/stop and shutter speed; the second by a contrast control symbol (N+1, N−2, etc.) and/or a paper grade number (#3, #2, whatever).

The back-up data can be kept on the Adams Exposure Record sheets (Morgan and Morgan), in a notebook, or by sketches. This includes meter readings, *placements*, *fall* of other values after placement, filters, factors, etc., whatever the reader needs.

A sketch in a notebook similar to the one shown greatly aids in learning to previsualize. Afterward, one can check plans, tonal predictions, and locate sources of error. *Treat the sketches as a learning device*; put them aside after their usefulness has passed.

The Arabic numbers inside the sketch refer to meter readings in light value numbers. The Roman numerals outside refer to zones. The underscored number stands for exposure *placement*. The rest refer to the print zones the photographer expects after the selected contrast control has been made.

**9.** Expose, process and print according to plan

The system is based on zones; and even after calibration and standardization (of processing), the first "standard print exposure" of any negative is only expected to put us within a zone of a fine print. And that only if no unforseen slip has occured such as a misfiring shutter. When the various values appear within the zone predicted, minimal manipulations generally assure a fine print. The seasoned zone system photographer has no qualms about "fine tuning" to produce a fine print. Ansel Adams com-

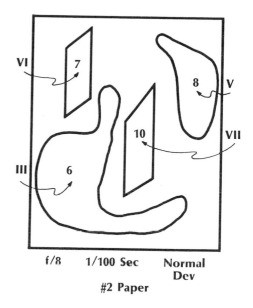

f/8    1/100 Sec    Normal Dev

#2 Paper

**Sketch for Recording Plans**

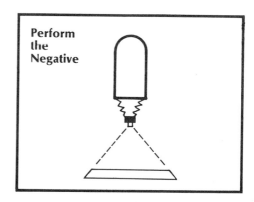

Perform the Negative

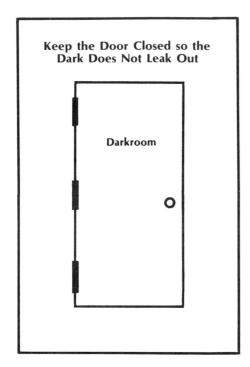

**Keep the Door Closed so the Dark Does Not Leak Out**

Darkroom

pares the negative to a musical score, and the print to a performance of that score. A better analogy of zone system printing can hardly be imagined.

To gain technical mastery, one sticks to the disciplines and performs the negative according to plan. Yet what is to prevent us from performing the negative any way inclination moves us? And yet again, many a negative has its own idea of how it must be printed! With growing discernment we can learn to be sensitive to the "wants" of negatives.

**10.** Compare final print to plan

Was the plan kept in mind while printing? (Postvisualization). Was the negative allowed to tell us how to print? Did we yield to an impulse? The experience of finding answers to these and similar questions may lead us to understand something of the strange process that goes on in us when we practice photography.

**11.** Back at the scene with the photograph

Comparing the present photograph with its original scene presents a fundamental challenge to our expectations of the medium. When we actually see how un-lifelike, how un-literal the Normal print is, how can we turn our back on the original, and again feel the photograph to be "true" to the subject? It is a tribute to our capacity to fool ourselves! "The camera never lies" is only half true. "The camera never tells the truth, either" is the other half. With such a confrontation regularly repeated, how do we approach the next photograph? As a challenge, of course. Taken as a challenge there is much to learn here for the next ten thousand photographs and at least one lifetime.

*Back at the scene, studying the photograph and checking our visualization. This is how we learn to make the next photograph.*

# Exposure-Control and Contrast-Control Options

As was said earlier, at step 7 or thereabouts, photographers can investigate any and all possible rendering, and a few impossible ones, so far as the immediate subject and moment goes. On this page plus two more we will summarize the major rendering possibilities of exposure-control combined with contrast-control. Other options, such as choice of film for renderings, we leave the reader to investigate.

### 1. Over-Scaled

*The subject or negative contrast range exceeds the print contrast range.*

A. *Expose for textured brights and let lower values lose texture or go black.*

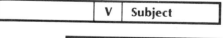

| | V | Subject |
|---|---|---|

| | | V | Film |
|---|---|---|---|

B. *Expose for the middle tones and let both ends lose texture.*

| | V | Subject |
|---|---|---|

| | V | Film |
|---|---|---|

*C. Expose for detail in shadows and let higher value go textureless white.*

| | V | Subject |
|---|---|---|

| | V | Film |
|---|---|---|

The present summary combines one type of rendering, low, middle and high key with another type, the relation of subject contrast range to optimum print gray scale: over-scaled, full-scaled, and under-scaled; in other words, high contrast prints, normal, and low contrast respectively. This particular set of options applies to controlled film exposure and variable film development, combined with negative exposure and various paper contrast grades. Note that the renderings depend on the willingness of the photographer to sacrifice parts of a subject or scene in order to emphasize some feature. Aesthetically satisfying photographs depend mostly on symbiotic relations between subject and optional rendering. Occasionally a subject or negative will yield satisfying pictures in two or three different renderings.

### 2. Full-scaled (Normal contrast range, 9, 10, 11 zones)

*Subject, negative, and print "match." The result is a full-substance (detail everywhere) and full-scale (Zone Zero through IX are present—so far as they exist in the original subject.)*

*High, middle, and low key depend entirely on distribution of tones in the subject.*

| | V | Subject |
|---|---|---|

| | V | Film |
|---|---|---|

### 3. Under-Scaled
The subject has fewer zones of contrast than the print scale.

| | V | Subject |
|---|---|---|

| | | V | Film |
|---|---|---|---|

A. Low Key
Expose the brights for Zone V or thereabouts, and let the rest disappear in black.

| | | V | Subject |
|---|---|---|---|

| | | V | Film |
|---|---|---|---|

B. Middle Key
Expose for the middle tones and be satisfied without either black or white.

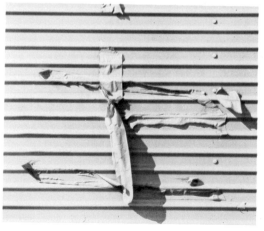

C. High Key
Expose for textured brights and nothing darker than about Zone V.

| | | V | Subject |
|---|---|---|---|

| | V | Film | |
|---|---|---|---|

# Field Demonstration of a Normal Photograph

By now the reader may want to dip into this system with camera and luminance meter. Admittedly, the instructions that follow pass lightly over a number of problems and say nothing about alternatives. Until the reader has made the calibrations, we have no other choice. So with a bow to the sun, we rest the success of the demonstration on the reader's good sense about field and darkroom practices.

### Directions for Demonstration

*Normal photographs usually assure a sense of space in depth, pervasive light and substance that corresponds quite well to these same three qualities in the original.*

Locate a scene or subject in which the shadow values placed in Zone III cause the high values to fall in Zone VII. (That in itself will give some practice in luminance meter technique.) Then you will need:

1. A Normal film developing time and dilution (see Appendix A).
2. A standard print exposure time for the negative. (To obtain a temporary print exposure time try this: find the minimum exposure time that prints the *blank edge* of the negative solid black. If sprocket holes are present, the black (Zone 0) of the blank edge should be almost black as the black in the holes; it never matches exactly.)
3. A Normal contrast grade of paper to enlarge on (#2 for large format negative, #3 for small).

Now proceed to meter, previsualize, expose, process and print according to the 10-step outline on the preceding pages.

The reader probably has his own expectations regarding the characteristics of a Normal photograph. So here is the main sign to look for. *Every value in the subject, regardless of zone, is REPRESENTED in the print.* As has been pointed out only a few of the print values are likely to exactly match the corresponding subject values, the rest, however, will be, as we say, "represented". Unless the reader has chosen to photograph, for example, a black-and-white checker board, Zones 0 through IX will appear in the print as if by magic.

The reader may not find open shadows, textured brights, and clear middle values in accord with his tastes. Not many people do today because the fashion in photographic rendering imitates magazine picture reproductions, and so is more contrasty than the zone system visual definition of Normal. Ansel Adams' prints are a prime example of what the "interpreted literal" aspect of the term Normal means visually. They are neither actually literal nor over-dramatized. They are just that degree between, to convince the viewer that had he or she stood beside the photographer at the moment of exposure, view and print would be identical.

During the demonstration the reader has been introduced to a processing standard of the system, though he-she may not have noticed it in passing. The standard is *print exposure time*, temporary though it be for now. In giving up the customary practice of compensating for overall negative density variations by adjusting print exposure times, we can become conscious of what different *film exposures* do alone. So, keeping print exposure constant, if the print seems too dark in general for Normal literalness, the *film* exposure was too short. If the print as a whole seems too light for Normal, the *film* exposure was too long. The discrepancy may be so obvious as to warrant a second session with the subject—altering film exposure appropriately, of course.

*When all is done and the reader-photographer is studying his Normal print, in case he does not ask, "What got demonstrated"? we will ask it now. Any number of discoveries may open, including the feeling that calibration is the next step, and due.*

*What was demonstrated?*

## Interface

When a photographer takes his photograph of Main Street back to Main Street, he can see, among other things, two sides or two ends of a problem he has solved. If he recalls the process between the two Main Streets, various activities come to mind: seeing, planning, exposing, printing, evaluating. Such activity between seeing the values in a subject and seeing the values in a photograph has various names. "Process" suggests craftsmanship with hands and tools, though the word does not lack mental implications. "Interface" lets us approach a familiar area from an unfamiliar point on the compass.

Interface means the common boundary between two surfaces, also the shared facts, theories, practices between two disciplines. In photography *interface* can be taken to mean ground common to three participants, subject, print, and photographer. (If we were concerned here with photography as communication, we would have to add the viewing audience as a fourth participant.)

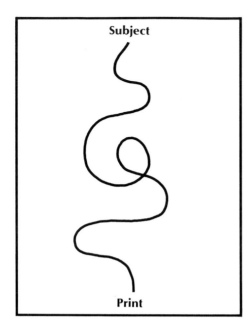

**Subject**

**Print**

**A**          **Interface**

If we think of original subject and derived photograph as the two goals of a hockey rink, how easy it is to see that the photographer's work corresponds to a game in progress.

Sketch A is a way of "speaking about" what goes on at interface when a craftsman-photographer "plays" (plans) a photograph. He or she can spend half an hour, a day, or a week working out a problem, and find most of it engrossing in progress and rewarding in completion. Whatever his discipline, it puts him in contact with the subject and sustains contact for long periods of time. But such a way of working is not as direct or intuitive as we have been led to expect of photography. Who will deny that "photos without bother" is an ideal in photography; and a dream camera, one that fits over the eyes like a pair of glasses and operates by a flick of an eyelash. Sketch B, next page, is a way of diagramming direct vision. Interface does not take place, or has been reduced to a straight line—or so it seems.

The snapshooter appears to bypass interface as if it did not exist. Holding the other end of the same stick are craftsmen-photographers who welcome interface, brief or extended. They "dig it" by whatever system they use, Kodak Handbook or Zone Book. Such craftsmen find that planning photographs, visualizing and all it implies, is creative work. Counting zones, exploring options and the like, actually IS contact with the subject. They "feel" their way into contact with the subject by mentally exploring its photographic possibilities. They report that deeper understandings can and do occur during their struggles with images on the groundglass to take advantage of exposure and contrast control by means of the luminance meter.

In the outline above, Steps 6 and 7 are creatively crucial because it is in this state that manipulating tones and zones can lead *through* the subject toward the creative. That possibility is always waiting during interface. Interface can be an active time-place continuum in the mental and psychological inner workings. But it is not always exercised. We can get so involved in planning, and even seeing, that any understanding of the subject does not surface into the conscious mind until some time later, when exposing, printing or evaluating the photograph. We recall three hours in an outdoor sculpture collection of ancient heads. We had packed our cameras and sat down to rest in the sun, facing the old Inca heads. Maybe we fell asleep. As we opened our eyes they were vibrantly alive; they had become living people standing in utter awe-vision of the sun.

For both ourselves and students we encourage "widening" interface rather than skipping it. Partly to make photographs that reflect our intentions, of course, but ultimately to provide a possibility and a means of becoming one with the subject. When that is the goal, manipulating zones and tones, values and scales, positives and negatives never deteriorate into finger exercises. Without such intentions realized, photographers begin to wonder why they continue with any conscious discipline.

The urge to let nothing interfere with seeing, certainly is not a stranger to the zone-systemized photographer. Making and sustaining contact with subjects intuitively is an experience that is always around in photography. So photographers who assimilate the system can learn to bypass interface as readily as a snapshooter, or so it seems.

Between casual snapshooters and creative photographers who take the casual seriously, there seems to be another interface. An "aesthetic of snapshot" has appeared which partakes of both immediate seeing and disciplined craft. The strongest of this school, Gary Winogrand, Lee Friedlander, Emmet Gowin, have a fine quality of perception. Perhaps they have always been intuitive, have always felt their way into the subject and reached a degree of penetration that zone system photographers earn by hard work. The latter, however, know something about what goes on in themselves during interface between Subject Values and Print Values. Being conscious of even a little of what goes on at interface is just the beginnings of research, and a full lifetime or two in the world of creativity.

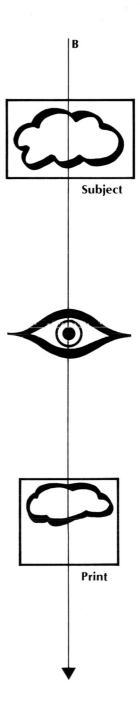

B

Subject

Print

# Calibration

Having acquired an inkling of the possibilities of the system, how do we gain positive control and make consistent photographs according to what we want? *Calibration* provides the standardization we must have to make previsualization predictable. The present procedure, though only one of several similar methods, offers a visual and quantitative technique that provides answers for typical zone system questions such as:

1. What exposure index should I use for my meter-film-developer combination?
2. What combination of time, temperature, developer, and developer dilution should I use to develop my film for Normal?
3. How do I determine the optimum exposure time for my printing paper?
4. How do I arrive at the Normal Minus development time that compensates for subject contrast of more than 10 zones? (Compactions.)
5. How do I find the development times that compensate for less than 10 zone subjects? (Expansions.)
6. How do I field test my calibrations?

As answers are found to these and other questions during calibration, we begin to make the system *our* Zone System. Personal standards begin to develop that are consistent with expressive purpose and the laws of sensitometry.

Each phase of calibration provides an opportunity to evaluate our methods and to change them in ways that will enhance technique and communication. Continued calibration will develop a repertory of different combinations of film, developers, papers and printing methods in keeping with the photographer's growth as a craftsman.

*Calibration amounts to the first practical step toward a view of photography as well-crafted medium.*

*The science of photography being what it is, all photographers use the Zone System whether they know it or not.*

48

The luminance meter is generally calibrated to a literal photograph (Normal) because that is convenient; the system photographer, however uses *normal* as a basis for planning, previsualizing and predicting *non-literal* photographs whenever that suits his purpose.

## Terminology

**Calibration Runs:** Standardizing exposure, development, and printing into a technically connected whole process. Four types are practiced. Each plays a certain part in the whole.

**Preliminary Run:** A diagnostic run at the rated film speed to arrive at an adjusted exposure index that takes into account individual equipment and processing variables. The true film speed is NOT changed. This run also determines the exposure basis for Zone I.

**Establishing Run:** To find Normal development for Zone V.

**Variable Development Runs:** To find Plus and Minus developments up to N−2 and N+2.

**Fine-Tuning Runs:** To find developer dilutions that will "hold" Zone I, and V "in place," and then bring VIII into "place" without loss of speed. (Excellent occupation for long rainy days and cold winter nights.)

**Adjusted Exposure Index:** An exposure adjustment set into the meter's film speed dial. Note especially that so doing does not alter the actual film speed. That is fixed at the factory.

**Exposure Zone or Exposure Value:** Segments or areas in the meter's exposure scale. A luminance reading is of little consequence until it is placed in an exposure zone on the meter. They are designated by Roman numerals.

**Flare:** Unwanted light within camera that affects Zone I and II adversely: plus stray light within enlarger that affects Zone VIII and IX adversely. Flare is to be especially avoided in calibration. Coated lenses reduce flare somewhat, but there are precautions that the photographer can take. See Appendix C.

**Reciprocity Effect:** When exposure time reaches one second or more, the normal response of film to light "falls off". It must be compensated for by additional exposure, and a comparable decrease in development. (See Appendix E for a table.) Any exposure series for calibration must avoid exposures of one second or longer.

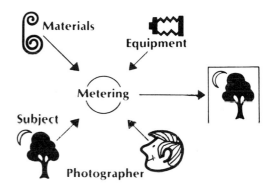

*When planning photographs calibration leads to visualizing the negative along with the positive.*

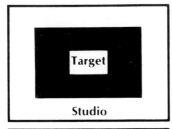

*Background*

Target

**Studio**

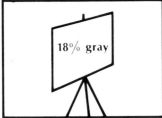

18% gray

*Gray Card Subject*

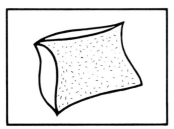

*Textured Subject*

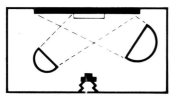

*Photofloods Floor Plan*

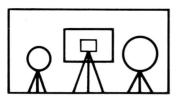

*Wall Plan for Light*

# Preparations

All the necessary materials should be on hand before you begin the calibration sequence, and your equipment thoroughly checked. Preparations are described in detail below.

## Calibration Materials

Background Cloth

A piece of dark, low-reflectance background material is used in making calibration exposures. Black velvet, reflecting only 1% of the light is ideal, however any dark material will do. It should be as large as possible to help keep stray light from entering the lens. (See Appendix C.) It serves as Zone 0 for the lower exposures.

Gray Card Subject

18% Neutral Gray Test Cards are available from camera stores, four 8X10 inch cards to a package. One is large enough for roll film exposures. Four taped together from behind make a single 16 X 20 inch target for sheet film exposures.

Textured Subject

In addition to the gray card, a textured subject is used for calibration exposures. The textured subject must be chosen carefully. Too much contrast is the danger, so terrycloth, or knitted wool, are suggested. In size it should be approximately 8 x 10 inches for roll film, or 16 x 20 for sheet film. Choose neutral or near-neutral colors, (medium gray). The more alike in reflectance the textured subject and gray card are, the less the photo-floods will have to be adjusted to obtain an equivalent exposure setting for Zone V.

Photofloods and Broad Reflectors

| Roll film: | Sheet film: |
|---|---|
| 2 — 4800K 250-watt daylight bulbs | 2—4800K 500-watt daylight bulbs |
| 2—10- or 12-inch reflectors | 2—12-inch reflectors |

Results obtained with 4800K daylight bulbs will be approximately equivalent to actual daylight conditions. Have four bulbs on hand, and change bulbs *long* before they burn out. (3200K bulbs will require ½-stop more exposure for results equivalent to 4800K bulbs.) Illumination on target must be even!

## Film Quantity

20 rolls or 50 sheets.

Fresh film with the *same emulsion number* should be used for calibration tests. Choose the film you use regularly, or a medium speed film (ASA 125) for initial testing. When the method is familiar, slower and faster films can be tested and calibrated as opportunity or need arises.

We suggest that roll film users standardize with the 20-exposure film developing reel, rather than the 36-exposure size because the development is more consistent from one end of the roll to the other.

*Film*
*Two factors promote more even development; the spirals in the 20-exposure reel are more widely spaced and so allow a greater flow of developer to film; the ratio of developer to film is almost twice that of the 36-exposure roll developed in the same 8-ounce tank.*

## Film Developer

Use a standard developer for calibration work. We recommend Kodak D-76 for roll film; Kodak HC-110 or Edwal FG7 for sheet film. *Calibration developer must not be replenished.* Stock solutions change characteristics much faster than developer concentrates diluted just before use. Make up stock in quart sizes. Fresh developer insures uniformity of results across successive calibration runs.

*Film Developer*
*For 35mm rolls use at least an 8 oz tank. For 120 rolls use at least a 16 oz. tank. For 4x5 sheets use at least a 32 oz tank (4 sheet maximum at a time). Large quantities of developer and good agitation insure uniform results.*

## Printing Paper

Printing papers from different emulsion batches show comparatively greater differences in contrast and speed characteristics than different film emulsions. For this reason it is a good idea to begin with an ample supply. Purchase paper in boxes of 100 sheets. Choose medium contrast, glossy, double-weight paper for initial calibration work. Additional contrast grades can be purchased in smaller quantity.

*Printing Paper*
*Make sure the paper is fresh. If in doubt, check the emulsion number with the manufacturer, or check expiration date.*

## Print Developer

Liquid concentrates diluted just before use will provide more consistent results than a stock solution used over the same period of time. Developers which come in powdered form should be mixed in small (one quart) quantities, dated, and used quickly. Always make up fresh working solution for each printing session. (Saved developer will not give the same results.)

*Print Developer*
*One quart of working solution is sufficient for printing a calibration run.*

*Notebook for recording runs and storing calibration negatives and prints*

Exposure Record Book

Use a large three-ring binder to store calibration negatives, prints, and exposure records for present use and *future reference*. Some of the "mistakes" will be exactly what is needed for a later run. So save all data, negatives and prints.

## Equipment Checks

### Light Meter

The zero setting of the light meter should be checked before using the meter to calculate exposures. Check the meter batteries and replace if necessary. CdS type meter cells should be exposed to moderate light for a few minutes before actual readings are made, to compensate for the meter's increased light sensitivity after being stored in the dark.

### Shutters

Shutters are a major source of variability in exposure. Have shutter speeds checked before beginning the calibration sequence. Then use only those speeds found to be accurate. Roll film users should avoid speeds higher than 1/125, and sheet film users speeds higher than 1/60 if possible. Shorter speeds can be avoided for the lowest zones by placing over the lens a 0.6 neutral density filter, equivalent to two f-stops less exposure. Speeds longer than one second should not be used in order to avoid film reciprocity drop-off. (See Appendix E)

### Thermometer

Before processing film, check your thermometer against a calibrated one if possible, or against at least two others considered accurate. If it appears to be off, replace it with a high quality thermometer accurate to within ½ degree.

# Basic Procedures

Before anything else, prepare an exposure record form. A model follows. The form should have twelve rows for 4 x 5-inch and 120 size formats, twenty rows for 35mm format.

## Calibration Exposure Record

| Film | | Developer | | Film Speed Index | |
|------|------|------|------|------|------|
| Frame Sheet | Exposure Number | Zone | f-Stop | Shutter | Subject |
| 1 | 1 | 0 | — | — | Lens Cap On |
| 2 | 2 | V | 8 | 1/30 | Gray Card |
| 3 | 3 | I | 22 | 1/60 | Textured |
| 4 | 4 | II | 16 | 1/60 | " |
| 5 | 5 | III | 11 | 1/60 | " |
| 6 | 6 | IV | 11 | 1/30 | " |
| 7 | 7 | V | 8 | 1/30 | " |
| 8 | 8 | VI | 5.6 | 1/30 | " |
| 9 | 9 | VII | 5.6 | 1/15 | " |
| 10 | 10 | VIII | 4 | 1/15 | " |
| 11 | 11 | IX | 4 | 1/8 | " |
| 12 | 12 | X | 4 | 1/4 | " |

Date: _____

Film: _____

Exposure Index: _____

Development: _____

Run: _____

The same basic procedure applies to all four types of calibration runs: Preliminary, Establishing, Fine-Tuning and Variable Development.

1. Target is pinned to dark background, **evenly illuminated.** The first target is the 18% gray card, focus on infinity. The second target is the textured subject in sharp focus.*
2. First target in place, photofloods are adjusted so that a Zone V exposure sets the shutter speed and aperture in the middle of their respective ranges. (When planning for the subsequent exposure series, always vary aperture settings instead of shutter speeds. Shutters are notoriously inconsistent.)
3. Make a series of exposures according to a plan. (Sample plans follow for all four types of run, as well as for 35mm, 120 and large format cameras.)
4. Process with calibration standards strictly adhered to.
5. Print according to standard procedures.
6. Evaluate.

For 10 or less frame exposure rolls, split the exposure series between two rolls. Expose excess frames to Zone V. Develop together in same tank.

* We suggest for view cameras that the lens be set at 2X focal length and multiply exposure by 4X. This is the easiest way to get accurate extension exposure increase.

# Preliminary Run

*The Preliminary Run aims at finding an effective film speed, and establishing Zone I.*

**The Four Calibration Runs:**

*Preliminary: to establish Normal Zone I and film Speed.*

*Establishing: to establish Normal Zone V.*

*Fine-tuning: to establish Normal Zone VIII and IX.*

*Variable Development: to establish Normal Minus and Normal Plus development times.*

*Vary f-stops rather than shutter speeds*

*We suggest that the photographer follow instructions without yielding to the short-cut temptations which will surely arise.*

*After the methods are established, by calibrating two or more films, safe short-cuts will suggest themselves.*

The instructions are detailed to save the photographer trouble. Much of what applies to the preliminary run applies to all the others, particularly the information on calibration processing, and on standard print exposure time.

1. Attach background cloth to a piece of firm cardboard taped to the wall. This makes it easier to pin and unpin targets.

2. Attach 18% gray card to background with push-pins.

3. Set up photofloods at 45° off camera axis on each side of the subject, same height as subject and 3-4 feet away.

4. We can not overstress **even illumination** of the subject.

5. For the preliminary run, set meter calculator for rated ASA film speed, or your usual exposure index.

6. Take a meter reading of the gray card target. Readings with spot meters (7° or less) can be taken from camera position. Readings with meters of a wider acceptance angle (15° or more) must be taken closer to the subject, approximately 7 inches from an 8 x 10 subject, or 14 inches from a 16 x 20 inch subject. In these cases great care must be taken *not to cast any shadows on the target.*

7. Adjust photofloods until a Zone V exposure is found that falls in the middle of the range of f-stop and shutter speed combinations for your camera. When using a film rated at ASA 125 we suggest the following Zone V indicated exposures.

   f/5.6 @ 1/60 for 35mm format
   f/8 @ 1/30 for 120mm format
   f/32 @ 1/15 for larger formats

These all avoid reciprocity fall-off. (See Appendix E)

8. Check again for evenness of illumination. Make sure that the Zone V exposure reading has not changed.

9. Enter the data in the exposure record. Zone V = shutter speed + aperture.

**10.** Predetermine the exposure combinations of f-stop and shutter speed for Zones I through IV, and then for Zones VI through X. A Zone 0 exposure is made with lens cap over the lens for roll film, or the dark slide in place for sheet film. Always *vary f-stop rather than shutter speed*, so far as possible. Enter exposure zone plan in the record, for example:

| Zone: | I | II | III | IV | V | VI | VII | VIII | IX | X |
|---|---|---|---|---|---|---|---|---|---|---|
| f-stop: | 16 | 11 | 8 | 8 | 5.6 | 4 | 4 | 2.8 | 2 | 2 |
| Shutter Speed: | $\frac{1}{125}$ | $\frac{1}{125}$ | $\frac{1}{125}$ | $\frac{1}{60}$ | $\frac{1}{60}$ | $\frac{1}{60}$ | $\frac{1}{30}$ | $\frac{1}{30}$ | $\frac{1}{30}$ | $\frac{1}{15}$ |

**11.** Begin the exposure series.
Below are instructions for three different film sizes, work with the one that applies.

## Exposure Instructions for 35mm Film

**1.** Load camera with film:
   **A.** Advance one frame after attaching film leader, release shutter, then close camera back.
   **B.** With the lens cap over the lens, advance film and release shutter three times. These frames receive no exposure. The last of these frames gives us a Zone 0 clear negative.
   **C.** The next exposure should correspond to Frame 2 on both the camera frame counter and the film itself.
**2.** Place camera on a tripod and position directly in front of, and close enough so that the gray card subject fills the entire viewfinder. With a normal lens the camera-to-subject distance will be approximately 12 inches.
**3.** Set the lens on infinity focus.
**4.** Referring to your exposure record, expose three frames:
   **A.** Expose Frame 2 to Zone I.
   **B.** Expose Frame 3 to Zone V (control print).
   **C.** Expose Frame 4 to Zone IX.
**5.** Remove gray card and replace with the textured subject.
**6.** Meter the textured subject and readjust the photofloods to obtain the identical Zone V exposure value as for gray card.

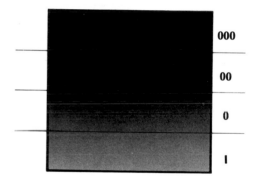

000

00

0

I

**Black includes several zones of darkness**

*The difference between Zone 0 and Zone I is barely noticeable. That is the way it is. Because of ink reproduction the difference between them is either too much or too little.*

*Doing calibrations by this visual method, the photographer learns about black. It is a whole group of zones extending into Zone 00, Zone 000, or darker. Zone I is a very narrow zone.* **55**

*Exposure Series: Roll Film*
*for Establishing and Fine-Tuning Runs*

| Expose Frame | to Zone | Target |
|---|---|---|
| 1 | 0 | Grey Card |
| 2 | I | |
| 3 | V | |
| 4 | IX | |
| 5 | I | Textured |
| 6 | II | Subject |
| 7 | III | |
| 8-14 | IV to X | |
| 14 | | |
| Remaining Frames | V | Grey Card or Textured Subject |

*With 10 frame rolls, or less, split exposures between two rolls. Expose remainder to Zone V. Develop the rolls together in same tank.*

7. Adjust camera-to-subject distance until the textured subject fills approximately one-third of the viewfinder. Center subject so that background frames it (with Zone 0). With a normal lens, an 8 x 10 inch subject would be photographed at a distance of 3-4 feet.

8. Focus the lens to obtain a sharp image in the viewfinder.

9. Referring to your exposure record, expose the next ten frames as follows:
   A. Expose Frame 5 to Zone I.
   B. Expose Frame 6 to Zone II.
   C. Expose Frame 7 to Zone III.
   D. Continue exposing Frames 8 through 14 to Zones IV through X.

10. Expose all the remaining frames to Zone V. This completes the exposure series. (Exposing all the frames simulates actual conditions of demand on developer. Exposing to Zone V produces an average density.)

11. Remove film in subdued light and label it.
    For example: Plus-X #1 @ ASA 125.

12. After processing and drying, cut film into convenient lengths for printing—*and later storage in notebook*—as follows:
    A. Frames 0 - 4    (Clear frames and gray card exposures)
    B. Frames 5 - 9    (Zones I through V of textured subject)
    C. Frames 10 - 14  (Zones VI through X of textured subject)
    D. Frames 15 - 19  (Zone V exposures to either textured subject or gray card)

    Prints from the control negatives (Zone V) are compared for possible exposure errors occasioned by changing from gray-card to textured subject, and moving lights.

    Processing directions are given on page 60.

**Exposure Instructions for 120 Film**
Similar to instructions for 35mm cameras except steps 1, 4, and 9 which have to do with exposure plan:

1. With lens cap over lens, advance film to Frame 1 and release shutter to produce Zone 0 negative.

4. Expose Frame 2 to Zone V, at infinity focus.

9. Expose next ten frames sequentially to Zones I through X, again according to plan for the exposure series.

## Exposure Instructions for Large Format Film

1. Load 12 sheets of film in film holders.
2. Number the film holders from 1 to 12.
3. Place camera on a tripod and position directly in front of the 16 x 20 inch gray card subject, close enough for its image to fill entire area of the groundglass.
4. Focus lens on infinity.
5. Pull darkslide halfway out of film holder. Referring to your exposure record, expose the uncovered half of Sheet 1 to Zone V. The covered, *unexposed* half corresponds to the Zone 0 clear negative.
6. Close darkslide, and turn the film holder to Sheet 2.
7. Remove the gray card and replace with the textured subject.
8. Meter the textured subject and readjust photofloods to obtain the identical Zone V exposure value used for the gray card.
9. Position the camera in front of the subject at a distance so that the subject fills approximately 2/3 to 3/4 the area of the groundglass. Background frame subject on all sides.*
10. Focus the image on the groundglass.
11. Observe the bellows extension. Use the same bellows extension for all future calibration runs to avoid possible errors in exposure. *Focusing can be done in subsequent runs by moving camera closer to or farther away from the subject.*
12. To calculate exposure correction factor for bellows extension, divide the square of the lens extension by the square of the focal length. $X = \dfrac{1 \, ext^2}{f^2}$ (Measure extension from film plane to diaphragm. Use inches or mm for *both* figures.)

    A factor of 1 requires no compensation.
    A factor of 1.5 requires an increase of ½ stop.
    A factor of 2 requires an increase of 1 stop.
    A factor of 3 requires an increase of 1½ stops.
    A factor of 4 requires an increase of 2 stops.

13. Before making any exposures, use data from step 12 to determine the corrected exposure combinations of f-stop and shutter speed for Zones I through X, and enter these values on your exposure record.

*Exposure Series: Sheet Film*

| Expose Sheet | to Zone | Target |
|---|---|---|
| 1 | 0 & V | Gray Card |
| 2 | I | Textured Subject |
| 3 | II | |
| 4 | III | |
| 5 | IV | |
| 6 | V | |
| 7 | V | |
| 8 | VI | |
| 9 | VII | |
| 10 | VIII | |
| 11 | IX | |
| 12 | X | |

First Tank

2nd Tank

*For view cameras set the lens at 2 X the focal length and multiply exposure by 4. For example, if the focal length of the lens (at infinity focus) is 3 inches, extend the bellows to 6 inches. (Measure extension from film plane to diaphragm of shutter.) Multiply indicated exposure X 4.*

**14.** Referring to the corrected values on your exposure record, expose Sheets 2 through 6 to Zones I through V.

**15.** Repeat the Zone V exposure on Sheet 7. (Sheet 7 is a control negative. Since only six sheets of film are to be developed at a time, two development runs are required. A comparison between the prints of Sheets 6 and 7, developed in two different runs will reveal any variation due to development.)

**16.** Expose Sheets 8 through 12 to Zones VI through X. This completes the exposure series.

## Processing the Calibration Negatives

*Standardization* of all processing chemicals and procedures is the secret of obtaining consistent and repeatable results.

In the Preliminary, Establishing, and Fine-Tuning calibration runs the only processing variables manipulated are film development time and developer dilution. The temperature, the *quantity* of solutions used, and the agitation are *standardized completely at the outset of the calibration sequence.*

Processing equipment such as tanks, reels, and measuring graduates should not be changed once the sequence is underway.

Choose a development temperature which is easy to maintain in your processing room. Most processing chemicals function best between 68° and 75°F.

If you plan to develop your film in a tank, fill the tank first, measure the developer temperature, then immerse the film.

The other chemicals should be premeasured and stored in containers kept in a tray of water to maintain constant temperature.

If you are developing roll film in stainless steel tanks, wear rubber gloves to prevent the heat of your hands from warming the developer. Then keep the tank in a water tray between agitation periods to insure constant temperature.

A consistent plan of agitation is essential for obtaining reliable results. Continuous agitation is used for tray development. A combination of continuous agitation for the first minute, followed by intermittent agitation is best for tank development.

*Alternative: put hand in cold water before grasping tank for agitation.*

*One good way of tray agitation is to divide the developer between two trays. Take film from bottom of pile (if developing two or more sheets) when transfering from one tray to the other.*

In tray development of sheet film, the films must be kept in constant motion by shifting their position from the bottom to the top of the pile, or from one pile to another. No more than six sheets should be developed at one time. Use a minimum of 64 oz. of fresh developer for every six sheets developed. 8 x 10 negatives should be developed one at a time in a minimum of 32 oz. of developer. (This helps keep temperature constant.)

Roll film developed in tanks should be agitated continuously for the first 30 seconds or 1 minute, by inverting the tank at the rate of 3 inversions in 5 seconds, followed by a gentle rap on the bottom of the tank to dislodge air bubbles. Then the tank should be inverted 3-5 times every 30 seconds (Kodak's recommendation), or 6-10 times every minute (as Ilford and Arnold Gassan recommend) for the remainder of development, with each agitation followed by the same gentle rap on the tank bottom.*

Sheet film developed by the tank method is agitated by lifting the film holders out of the developer, tipping them to one side, immersing them in the developer, removing them again, tipping the film holders to the other side, then reimmersing them in the developer. This constitutes one complete cycle of agitation.

Develop the Preliminary Calibration Run for your customary development time, or use the film manufacturer's recommended time for normal contrast.**

These recommendations are for average contrast scenes which are intended to be printed on normal contrast printing paper. Negatives processed to Ilford's specifications will require one grade *lower* contrast paper than negatives processed to Kodak's specifications.

Avoid overfixing film or printing paper, particularly with rapid fixing formulas which will dissolve some of the silver deposited on the negative or print, resulting in a loss of shadow detail and apparent film speed with negatives, and a loss of deep black print values in prints.

## Agitation Plans for Tank Development

In all plans keep agitation constant for first minute.

### Plan 1
*Up to 5 min.*
*constant*

### Plan 2
*5-10 min.*
*15 sec. per minute*

### Plan 3
*10-20 minutes*
*30 sec. per minute*

### Plan 4
*20 minutes and up*
*30 sec. per 2 minutes up to 20 minutes*
*60 sec. per 5 minutes up to 60 minutes*
*60 sec. per 10 minutes over 60 minutes*

*Use a "torus" motion when developing in a tank for even results. "Torus" is a quasi-spiral movement.

** Kodak recommends developing their films to Contrast Index values of 0.45 and 0.56 for condenser and diffusion enlargers respectively. Ilford, using a similar *average gradient* ($\bar{G}$) system recommends a $\bar{G}$ of 0.5 and 0.70 for condenser and diffusion enlargers respectively. (See Appendix B).

A simple film clearing time test: Place an unexposed strip or sheet of film directly into fixer. Under a safe-light check how long it takes the film to clear. *Double* this time for fixing. Prints clear in about half the time of most films.

Always process prints in fresh developer with a standardized time, temperature, quantity, and dilution.

Always develop calibration prints for 3 minutes at 70°F, with constant agitation during development, stop bath, and fixing.***

**Any print you are serious about deserves the same treatment.**

*\*\*\*Develop Resin Coated (RC) papers for 1½ minutes at 70° F. Agitation constant through all baths.*

## Printing the Calibration Negatives

*Printing must be as standardized as film processing.*

Printing the calibration negatives must be as standardized as film processing. Print the calibration negatives identically; then the differences in print values may be attributed to the negatives and not to printing variables. So exposure time, and developer quantity, dilution and temperature must be held constant. To print calibration negatives, a *standard print time* is required. Standard print time is determined as described below. This standard takes into account variations due to enlarger, film, and printing paper characteristics. Standard print time is defined as the minimum exposure time for any given paper to render a Zone 0 negative as a pure black print value.

### Instructions for Determining Standard Printing Time

*Instructions for Standard-Printing-Time*

1. Set enlarger height for 8 x 10 or whatever enlargement ratio you use most frequently.
2. Insert clear (Zone 0) negative in the negative carrier and focus the edge of the carrier on the easel.
3. Set the lens aperture on f/11, or your usual setting for printing normal contrast negatives.
4. Make Standard Black and White Patches:
   A. Expose a 4 x 5 piece of printing paper for 1 minute then develop it according to a standard method (usually 3 minutes at 70°F). This is the maximum black obtainable with this paper. For exceptions (see Appendix K Selenium Toning.)

**B.** Without exposing it, develop a 4 x 5 piece of printing paper. This is the maximum white obtainable with this paper. When fixed, store both in fresh water.

5. With the easel centered under the enlarger light, expose a 4 x 5 piece of paper in five two-second exposures, successively covering one inch of the paper after each exposure. Then uncover it and expose the entire paper for four seconds. Thus this "step wedge" will have exposures of 6, 8, 10, 12 and 14 seconds.

6. After standard processing, examine the step wedge print under direct light* (100-watt bulb in a reflector 15 inches away). If all the steps turn out gray, open your enlarging lens one stop and repeat the test. If all the steps are black, close down your enlarging lens one stop and repeat.*

7. To determine standard print exposure time, locate the first step of the wedge which is completely black (Zone 0) and at the same time is adjacent to the last discernible dark gray step (Zone I). Keep comparing with the standard black patch. Take the exposure time of this critical black step as the standard print exposure time—at that enlarging ratio.

8. Expose a 4 x 5 print to the enlarger light at standard print time. Label it Zone 0. When the prints are dry, compare this Zone 0 print with the dried black patch.

9. Use this combination of enlargement ratio, printing paper, standard exposure time, and development to print all the remainder of the calibration negatives. No exceptions!

10. During Step 9, write the exposure zone of each negative on the back of its corresponding print. Use a soft pencil.

11. When dry, lay the prints out in the form of a zone ruler, and begin the evaluation.

## Evaluating the Preliminary Run

Evaluating the preliminary run is likely to tax the judgement of any photographer trying to work exclusively out of a book. To offset the absence of a teacher, much data follows—including the (hopefully helpful) print zone ruler on the back cover.

*Critical is the first separation of dark gray from black. (See page 57)*

* *This intensity of illumination is ideal. Rarely are photographs seen in that much light, so the 100-watt bulb could be used at 3 feet. However, a loss of black is the result. Experiment with the difference.*

*Evaluating Preliminary Run (Zone I)*

*The aim is an **adjusted** film speed index that takes into account equipment, materials, lens flare, and personal processing habits. When found, it is generally called **effective film speed.***

*A verbal description of a 9 zone print scale appears in the main text. Since 9, 10 and 11 zone scales are in use for Normal these days, a verbal description follows of a 10 zone scale. The two descriptions may help in evaluating the preliminary run.*

If you exposed and developed your preliminary run at the manufacturer's rated ASA index and development time, and printed the negatives on normal contrast paper, you can anticipate the following approximate print values:

Zone I, pure black, Zone IX, pure white;
Zone II, the first separation in tone from pure black;
Zone VIII, the last separation from pure white; and
Zone V, approximate equivalent to the 18% neutral gray card: in short a nine-zone scale.*

**0** Maximum black.
**I** A slight but noticeable separation in tone from Zone 0 black, when viewed under direct light.
**II** The first appearance of texture.
**III** The first fully-textured print value.
**IV** Textured dark gray.
**V** Textured middle gray (equivalent to the 18% neutral gray card).
**VI** Textured light gray.
**VII** The last fully-textured print value.
**VIII** The last appearance of texture.
**IX** A slight threshold gray merging into whiteness of the paper base.

(Practically, Zone IX is white paper.)

The zone system originally took a 10-zone scale as the standard Normal: Lately, sophisticated photographers use 9, 10 and 11 zone scales for Normal.

To begin evaluation of the first run, the two control frames are compared: the Zone V print of the gray card is compared to the Zone V print of the textured-subject. *Squinting helps.* They should be approximately equal in tone since both were exposed to Zone V. If not, something went wrong. (Roll film users can anticipate the grey card print being less than ½-zone lighter, because no compensation was made for lens extension.)

A larger difference in tone (more than ½-zone) suggests possible errors in metering, adjustment of the lights or, on large format cameras, compensation for bellows extension. If this happens, the test should be repeated after checking all possible sources of error. The new Zone V control prints should be compared again until an approximate match is achieved.

### Zone I Evaluation: Adjusted Exposure Index

To find the correct exposure index for the 10 zone scale, examine the dark end of the zone ruler. Under direct light, locate the first print which shows a slight separation in tone between subject and background (Zone 0). Call this print Zone I. Turn it over to see what exposure zone is written on the back. If its negative *was* exposed to Zone I, the correct exposure index was used in exposing the film; if not, a correction is in order. The table of adjustments below is based on a rated film speed of 100. Adjustments are made by appropriately changing the number in the film speed window on the meter to a new exposure index.

* The unofficial normal contrast negative of the photo industry appears to be a nine-zone scale. This accounts for slightly contrasty prints when following manufacturer's directions. Adams on this problem says that zone system calibration employs a single-toned target, which gives different results than averaging the tones of a multi-toned subject.

**Evaluating Preliminary Run**

| Assumed Zone I actually exposed to | Adjust to | |
|---|---|---|
| I | 100 | no adjustment (ASA) |
| II | 50 | ½ original index |
| III | 25 | ¼ original index |

Some "Zone I's" will fall between. For example if the assumed Zone I is more than a *slight* separation, but still not a textured print value, the rated index was ½-stop too low. Adjust exposure index accordingly at 150 (ASA x 1.5).

## Zone V and Zone IX Check

From the correctly adjusted Zone I print in the new zone ruler, count four zones to the right. This would be the print value obtained for a Zone V exposure at the *adjusted* exposure index. Compare this print with the 18% gray card itself. If it is lighter, decrease development. If it is darker, increase development in the next run.

To "raise" or "lower" Zone V by one zone, increase or decrease development times 30-40% for high speed films (ASA 400), 20-30% for medium speed films (ASA 125), and 15-20% for low speed films (ASA 32-50).

If Zone V is off, the upper zones of your exposure series are likely to be even further off than Zone V, thus verifying the need for a change of development time. Compare the adjusted preliminary zone ruler to the one on the back cover of the manual. This will help in evaluating development adjustment.

*Reproduction of three tests made with a textured target. A approximates a N + 2 test, B approximates a Normal, C approximates a N − 2. The tests were based on Zone V instead of Zone I. Consequently, except for Zone V in each scale, all the other "Zones" vary in unexpected ways. Visualization must take these variations into account when planning photographs. See the chart on page 88 that concerns Bi-Directional Contrast-Control for further explanation; and page 102 for sensitometric graphs of corresponding paper scales.*

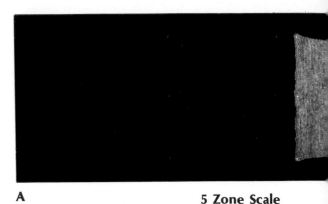

**A**                    **5 Zone Scale**

**B**                    **9 Zone Scale**

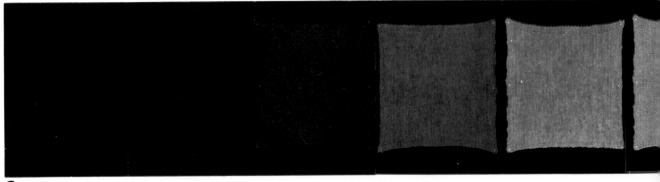

**C**                    **11 Zone Scale**

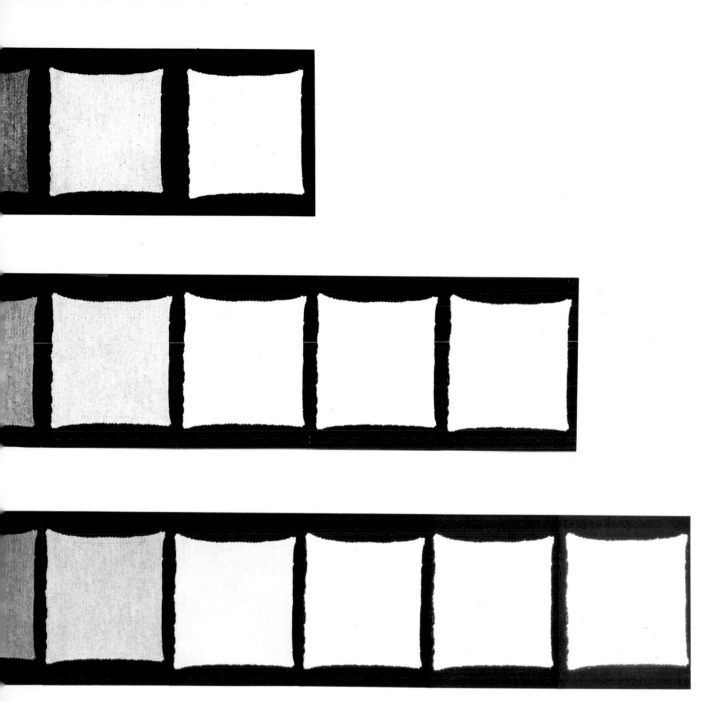

65

# The Establishing Run for Normal Development

Once you have determined an adjusted exposure index for Zone I and have estimated the development time for Zone V, you are ready to begin an Establishing Run.

If you are using an exposure index different from your Preliminary Run, use the **same exposure settings of f-stop and shutter speed,** but **vary the light intensity** of the photofloods to obtain the same indicated Zone V exposure value.*

The exposure series for the Preliminary and Establishing Runs are identical. Follow the same instructions given earlier. Use the new exposure index (effective film speed), and the estimated development time for film. Print negatives at standard print exposure time, in fresh developer.

### Evaluating the Establishing Run

Begin by squinting at the Zone V *gray card* print next to the Zone V *textured subject* print to check reliability of the exposure sequence. If no exposure errors were made these prints will match.

Lay out the new prints of the textured subject in zone ruler form. Starting with the *adjusted* Zone I, lay out the Preliminary Run prints above the new prints, zone for zone.

Zones I through III should be approximately equal in print value on both zone rulers. Then, beginning at Zone IV, the effects of a change in development should be apparent. Zone IV and above will be lighter with more development, darker with less.

Compare the Establishing Run Zone V prints of both the gray card and the textured-subject with the actual gray card. An approximate match indicates that you have achieved a normal development time. (If these prints are still lighter or darker than the gray card by more than ½-zone, make a new run and change development time appropriately.)

Compare the upper zones with the zone ruler on the back cover of the book. They may be off more than ½-zone. If so, this is where fine-tuning enters.

*Aim of the establishing run is to verify normal Zone V.*

* *A lower exposure index will require moving the photofloods closer to the subject than in the last run. A higher exposure index will require moving the photofloods farther away from the subject. Roll film users may wish to substitute daylight bulbs of higher wattage (500 watts) if more light intensity is needed at the adjusted exposure index.*

# Fine-Tuning Runs

With some film and developer combinations, it is possible to have a correctly exposed Zone I, a correctly developed Zone V, and at the same time, Zones VII through IX that print too light or, in some instances, too dark.

If development time alone is used to raise or lower these upper zones, the Zone V calibration will be sacrificed. If, on the other hand, the developer *dilution* is manipulated, *the contrast of Zones VII-IX can be increased or decreased while maintaining the calibration of Zones I through V. Varying the dilution of the developer to control contrast above Zone V is called "fine-tuning."*

To estimate what dilution to use, refer to the renditions of Exposure Zone VIII. Compare the prints of your Establishing run with the Zone ruler on the back cover. If Zone VIII is rendered as Zone IX (approximately), try a 1:2 dilution. If Exposure Zone VIII is rendered as Zone VII (approximately), it will be necessary to start over with either a more powerful developer or a lower dilution. (Developers have, so to speak, different degrees of contrast. In a series D-23 is the lowest, then progressively more "contrasty" D-76, FG-7, and HC110.)

The table below shows development time changes when D-76 or similar developers are diluted with a medium speed film.*

*The aim of fine-tuning is to control the contrast of Zones VIII and IX while keeping Zones I and V "in place," that is, Normal.*

*Dilutions work best with Normal developments.*

**Fine-tuning** *by developer dilutions was absent from previous editions of the Zone System Manual, and only recently have we looked into this possibility. So the data included are guidelines at best. We have studied the dilution effects for only four developers: Kodak D-76, D-23, HC-110, and Edwal FG7. Application of the general effects probably holds with other developers of similar composition; to what extent, the reader-photographer can only determine by testing.*

| Developer Dilution From mfr's recommended working solution | Development Time Change (Approximate) | Exposure-Zone V Rendered | Exposure-Zone VIII Rendered (Approximate) | Example |
|---|---|---|---|---|
| Working Solution | None | V | IX | 6 min. |
| 1:1 | 25% increase | V | VIII½ | 7½ min. |
| 1:2 | 50% increase | V | VIII | 9 min. |
| 1:3 | 75% increase | V | VII½ | 10½ min. |
| 1:4 | 100% increase | V | VII | 12 min. |

*High speed films require approximately 40-50% more development for each increase in dilution. Slow speed films require somewhat less than indicated in table. The table does not hold for concentrates such as FG7.

*Evaluating the Fine Tuning Runs
Compare the Zone 1
of the Fine-Tuning Run with
Zone 1 of the Establishing Run.*

*Compare the Zone V
with the Zone V
of the Establishing Run.*

*Compare Zone VIII with
the Zone VIII on the back cover.
Or compare visually with
the following verbal description:
Zone VIII is slightly, but slightly,
darker than white Zone IX.*

Whenever you change the dilution and make a Fine Tuning run, check the Zone I print of the new series against the Zone I of the Establishing Series to determine if any change in film speed has occurred. *Higher* than normal dilutions may result in a slight *loss*, while *lower* than normal dilutions may result in a slight *increase* in film speed. Either condition can be compensated for by a ½-stop or so change in exposure index in the appropriate direction.

## Recommendations Based on Empirical Investigations

Dilute developers are recommended particularly for roll film because the negative densities of the upper zones must be rigorously controlled to avoid graininess and blocked highlights in prints.

The following dilutions of D-76 are suggested for *Normal* development of roll film: 1:2 for high speed films (ASA 400), 1:3 for medium speed films (ASA 125), and 1:4 for low speed films (ASA 32-50). These dilutions at normal development produce somewhat less than normal contrast above Zone V, insuring textured print values in Zones VII and VIII.

**Recommended Dilutions of D-76 or D-23 for Roll Film Development**

| Film | Development Effect | Straight | Dilution 1:1 | 1:2 | 1:3 | 1:4 |
|------|--------------------|----------|--------------|-----|-----|-----|
| Low Speed ASA 32-50 | N− | D-76 D-23 | D-76 D-23 | | | |
| | N | | | D-23 | D-76 D-23 | D-76 |
| | N+ | D-76 | D-76 | | | |
| Medium Speed ASA 125 | N− | D-23 D-76 D-23 | D-23 D-76 D-23 | | | |
| | N | | | D-23 | D-76 D-23 | D-76 |
| | N+ | D-76 | D-76 | | | |
| High Speed ASA 400 | N− | D-23 D-76 D-23 | D-23 D-76 D-23 | | | |
| | N | | | D-76 D-23 | D-76 D-23 | |
| | N+ | D-76 D-23 | | | | |

*Straight means the working solution recommended by the manufacturer (undiluted, full-strength).*

*The appearance, for example, of D-76 in both the straight and 1:1 column means that either dilution will give satisfactory compactions and expansions, though the times will be different.*

The following dilutions of either Kodak HC-110 *stock* or Edwal FG7 *concentrate* are suggested for Normal development of sheet film: 1:3 for higher than normal contrast above Zone V; 1:7 for normal contrast; and 1:15 for less than normal contrast above Zone V.

**Recommended Dilutions of Edwal FG7\* and Kodak HC-110\*\* for Sheet Film Development**

| Film | Development effect | Dilution\*\*\* | | | |
|---|---|---|---|---|---|
| | | 1:3 | 1:7 | 1:15 | 1:31 |
| Low Speed ASA 32-50 | N− | | | FG7<br>HC-110 | HC-110 |
| | N | | | FG7<br>HC-110 | |
| | N+ | | FG7<br>HC-110 | FG7<br>HC-110 | |
| Medium Speed ASA 125 | N− | | | FG7<br>HC-110 | HC-110 |
| | N | | FG7<br>HC-110 | FG7<br>HC-110 | |
| | N+ | | FG7<br>HC-110 | FG7<br>HC-110 | |
| High Speed ASA 400 | N− | | | FG7<br>HC-110 | HC-110 |
| | N | | FG7<br>HC-110 | FG7<br>HC-110 | |
| | N+ | FG7<br>HC-110 | FG7<br>HC-110 | | |

\*FG7 Concentrate    \*\*HC-110 Stock

A procedure for testing is now completed, and a method established.

Apply it with appropriate modifications to future testing: expansions and compactions, special developers and films, filters and pre-exposure.

The degree of accuracy obtainable, lying as it does between scientific accuracy and happy accident, serves the medium of pictorial photography very well.

### Get Acquainted with Mode Normal

*Adjusted exposure index verified, standard print time found, normal development established, we are prepared to explore normal as a mode of expression. Practice will produce a feeling for full-scale, ten-zone photographs. Nothing else will. So practice until normal contrast subjects and scenes can be spotted without using a meter. Patience to stay with the mode until acquaintance is made will be well rewarded. Familiarity takes longer, and mastery takes. . .?*

*According to students, experiencing calibration involves many emotions: chagrin at careless processing habits, satisfaction with improved technique, discovery that the negative can be visualized along with the future photograph, amazement at how many variables calibration unifies.*

\*\*\*At a given dilution, contrast-control can be obtained by changing *time* only. Conversely, at a given development time, contrast-control is possible by changing *dilution* only. However, compactions by dilution only lead to a considerable loss in effective film speed, and are therefore NOT recommended.

## Contrast Control:
### By Variable Film Development and Various Paper Contrast Grades

The method of testing presented in the preceding pages on Normal development will be applied throughout this section. Notice a feature of the method: *once the normal zone ruler is established, it is used for comparison thereafter.* As we will see shortly, after various developments, certain critical zones are compared to predetermined zones in the Normal zone ruler. For example: a number of Zone V exposures are developed at different times; then the one that matches Zone VI is taken as N+1. This will become clear as we make the Expansion and Compaction calibrations.

Contrast control in photography is by no means limited to film development and paper grades. Exposure itself affects the contrast of the lower zones. Appendix F shows this control by means of graphs and curves. Several other means are available. On a scale of effectiveness, studio lighting runs high; pre-exposure is limited to contrasty scenes, filters to increasing contrast; burning and dodging affect local contrast; fill-in flash overcomes flare in backlighted subjects. Two-solution film developers have little effect on modern super-thin emulsions; but two-bath print developers make fine-tuning prints a joy. Last, but not least, there is the contrast control of waiting for the light to change. That is the only control available with automatic cameras, Polaroid, and color transparency material in any camera. Though hardly popular, waiting for light to shift on the subject to alter the contrast range does put one in touch with the magic of light. On days of alternating sun and clouds the photographer may even see how luck influences his or her work. By contrast, studio contrast control involves changing bulb wattages and moving light stands, but no waiting! Moving lights, like waiting, becomes a part of creative action, each with its unique ritual of involvement.

Two terms need to be brought to the attention of the reader, *overall contrast* and *local contrast.* The first means the contrast range over the entire negative or print. The second means the contrast range found in its smaller local areas.

*Local contrast in shade is identical with local contrast in sun. Each implies expansion, but together, the overall contrast requires compaction.*

*Local contrast plays an important part in planning photographs. One often asks questions such as, "Must the visible contrast in the shadows be sacrificed for the sake of overall contrast?" and "What contrast control is needed to keep skin and flesh values in the middle zones without losing at both ends?"*

## Contrast Control by Various Paper Grades*

The development designations N−1, N+1, etc. have already been applied to subject contrast ranges and are here extended to paper grades. The table below shows the approximate correlations between development symbols and paper grades. As will be seen, film developments give somewhat more control than paper grades.

**Based on a 10-zone, black through white, scale**

| Film | | Paper | |
|---|---|---|---|
| **Development** | **will render** | **Grade** | **will print** |
| N+2 | 8 zone subject as full scale | #5 | 8½ zones as full scale |
| N+1 | 9 zone subject as full scale | #4 | 9¼ zones as full scale |
| N | — | #3 | Full scale print |
| N−1 | 11 zone subject as full scale | #2 | 10½ zones as full scale |
| N−2 | 12 zone subject as full scale | #1 | 11 zones as full scale |

An intriguing thought occurs; paper contrast grades alter the effective contrast of the negative only for each print; different film developments permanently alter the contrast.

### Determination of Paper Contrast Symbols by the Photographer

American and European manufacturers have not standardized their numbering systems or the contrast range covered by their graded papers. Sometimes contrast grades are not evenly spaced within the same brand and type of paper. Consequently calibrations are in order.

To calibrate the N+ or N− effects of grades higher or lower than normal contrast paper, proceed as follows:

1. Print your calibrated Zone VII *negative* of the textured subject on each grade of paper available. (#1 through #5 if possible). Adjust exposure for each paper grade to match the calibrated

*FINE-TUNING STANDARD PRINT TIME:*

*With increasing frequency these days a new supply of printing paper will not give the same results as the paper used in your original calibration. Differences in both* **contrast** *and* **speed** *often occur*

*To cope with these variations, we must find an adjusted Standard Print Time for each new box of paper used. Take your calibrated normal Zone V grey card negative and adjust the print time to match the Zone V print on your original printing paper. This becomes the new Standard Print Time.*

*Then, at the adjusted printing time, print your calibrated Zones II and VIII negatives on the new paper and compare these prints to your original calibrated prints.*

*If the new Zone II is darker, and the Zone VIII print is lighter than the original prints, the new paper is more contrasty. If, on the other hand, the new Zone II print is lighter, and the Zone VIII print darker, the new paper is less contrasty.*

* See Appendix H

**Printed for sky with #1 filter**

**Printed for foreground with #4 filter**

**Lower part printed with #4 filter**
**Upper part printed with #1 filter**

Zone VII *print*. Note exposure time and grade on the back of each matching print. Eliminate those that do not match.

2. Print your calibrated Zone III negative at the same time found for the Zone VII negative, grade for grade. For example, if grade #5 took 18 seconds to produce the Zone VII matching print, expose the Zone III negative on grade #5 for exactly the same time.

3. Compare the Zone III prints to your Normal contrast ruler thus:
The Zone III print that matches V indicates N−2
The Zone III print that matches IV indicates N−1
The Zone III print that matches III indicates N
The Zone III print that matches II indicates N+1
The Zone III print that matches I indicates N+2

Now armed with reliable data on your paper grades, paper speeds, and relation to contrast control symbols, you are prepared to fine-tune prints into well-crafted photographs.

**Fine-Tuning with Paper Grades and Developers**
For every grade of paper you intend to use, also determine a standard print time, thus setting a Zone 0 (clear) negative at maximum black. (A method was given on page 62.) Such determinations will provide a *speed factor* between paper grades. (As you may recall, for any given contrast grade of paper, less than standard print time exposure will eliminate black; more exposure will submerge shadow detail.)

**A Test Strip Technique**
A test strip technique has been devised that extends its use beyond exposure considerations alone. If used in a specific way it will indicate which grade of paper will produce the normal full-scale print. The procedure follows:

1. Cut 3 same-sized test strips of normal grade paper. They can vary in size, 1'' wide by 4'' long, 6'' long, 8'' long, etc. depending on enlargement and how far apart the darkest and lightest areas are on the easel.

2. Position them one at a time so that the darkest areas and the lightest areas of the projected negative are *both* on each strip.

3. Expose one at the standard print time.
   Expose the second 5 seconds more.
   Expose the third 5 seconds less.
   Develop all three together.

4. Check the Zone VII-VIII areas:
   Note exposure time of strip showing texture in VII-VIII. If none shows, make new test strips, exposed at 2X, 4X, 8X the time of the darkest strip. Select the time that shows texture.

5. Observe the shadow areas:
   If Zone III is present and textured, normal paper is right.
   If Zone III is in II or lower (no texture), a change to an N−1 or N−2 paper is indicated.
   If Zone III is in IV or V, a change to N+1 or N+2 paper is indicated.

6. Make a "work" print of the whole negative on the indicated paper grade. Expose at what appears to be the best print time.

7. Then check local contrasts (Zones III through VII) for texture. Test local plus and minus changes with local test strips, and start toward a final fine print.

   **A. First Test Strip**
   Includes darkest and lightest areas.
   On a #3 paper, all the exposures were too light.
   **B. Second Test Strip**
   8 times exposure of the first, on a #3 paper
   Tonalities in the light areas suggest ½ as much exposure.
   Lack of detail in shadows suggests a #2 paper.
   **C. First Work Print**
   Made according to estimates of exposure and paper grade from the 2nd test strip.
   The result is approximately a Normal Print.
   Further tonal changes, local or overall, more or less contrast, as well as cropping can be determined by a study of this print.

## Another Method: Standard Print Times

In place of the familiar test strips, standard print times may be used to indicate which grade of paper will produce a full-scale (ten-zone) print; here is how. When printing a negative, if the best exposure time for important subject values is *less* than standard printing time of a particular paper, use the next *higher* contrast grade. If the best exposure time is *more* than standard printing time, use the next *lower* paper grade.

*A test strip technique for reading both print exposure and paper grade.*

**A**        **Test Strip**        **B**

**Work Print**
**C**

As we know, paper from grade to grade provides about 1/2 to a 3/4-zone change in contrast. Fine-tuning generally explores possibilities *within* the local contrast range of the various zones. Other contrast control such as shortening print development time (or lengthening it) has only a slight effect, especially on those papers that respond to prolonged development, not by increasing contrast but by increasing overall density. A more effective process consists of two baths, the first solution is a low contrast developer (Kodak Selectol Soft for example), the second high contrast (Kodak Dektol). The two solutions may be mixed to form a single bath, or kept in separate trays and the prints developed at different times in each bath.

Here is a table of mixtures from *stock* solutions of low contrast (soft), high contrast (hard) developer, and water. Each combination totals 16 parts. The dilution is approximately 1:1.

|  | N+ |  |  |  | N |  |  |  | N− |
|---|---|---|---|---|---|---|---|---|---|
|  |  |  |  |  | Parts |  |  |  |  |
| Soft | 0 | 1 | 2 | 3 | 4 | 5 | 6 | 7 | 8 |
| Hard | 16 | 7 | 6 | 5 | 4 | 3 | 2 | 1 | 0 |
| Water | 0 | 8 | 8 | 8 | 8 | 8 | 8 | 8 | 8 |

The difference between *Soft* straight and *Hard* straight is under two zones. The 4-4-8 mix is taken as Normal. The mixed solutions give a brilliance in print quality not quite matched by the two-bath method, so use them for fine prints.

Use the two bath technique for proofing: Soft developer is followed by Hard developer.

|  | N+ |  | N |  | N− |
|---|---|---|---|---|---|
| Soft | 30 sec. | 60 sec. | 90 sec. | 2 min. | 2½ min. |
| Hard | 2½ min. | 2 min. | 90 sec. | 1 min. | 30 sec. |

Further refinement is gained by varying the dilution of the hard and soft developer, straight, 1:2, 1:3, etc. When the two solution technique is added to paper grades (or the filters of variable contrast papers), fine-tuning becomes amazingly subtle and extensive.

## Contrast Control Through Variable Film Development*

Sensitometrists discovered long ago that contrast control through film development stems from a unique characteristic: development increases the density in the slightly exposed regions of the film far less than in the thoroughly exposed regions. Thus as development time lengthens, the negative density range is expanded and contrast increased. Between the usable limits of long and short development lies a norm.

Zones IV, V, and VI serve best for expansion studies. Zones VII, VIII and IX for compaction studies. We take Zone V as the base for expansions and Zone VII as the base for compactions; Zone V because throughout the book it is used as the pivotal zone; Zone VII because we want to know how much less development is necessary to bring a subject value falling beyond the range to within the range of fully-textured print values. Zone VII is taken to be the upper limit of fully-textured print values under normal development conditions. If you later find that some base other than V and VII is desirable, the method given below needs only minor modifications.

## Expansion Calibrations:

### N+1 Calibration

To find a starting point for an N+1 expansion, increase your Normal development time 30-40% for high speed films (ASA 400), 20-30% for medium speed films (ASA 125), and 15-20% for low speed films (ASA 32-50).

**1.** Expose the textured subject as you did in the Calibration sequence to Zones I through VIII at your calibrated exposure index. Develop the negatives at the estimated N+1 time and print all negatives on normal contrast paper at the standard print time.

**2.** Then compare the N+1 prints with your calibrated normal contrast prints by laying out both sets of prints to form two parallel zone rulers. First look for any differences in Zones I through III. The effective film speed increases slightly with increased develop-

*As has been said, contemporary films, (mid-1970's) are multilayered and very thin. Consequently contrast control by variable film development is more restricted than formerly. N+2 and N−2 are approximately the limits, and that depends on the thickness or thinness of the emulsions. Thick emulsions permit more contrast control.*

*Expansion calibration is arbitrarily based on Zone V. It could be just as well based on Zone VIII. The two different bases require different development times. It takes more time to reach N+1 "raising" V to VI than raising VII to VIII, and the effect on the higher zones is more pronounced in the former.*

ment, though usually no correction will be needed for an N+1 expansion.

**3.** Compare the *expanded Zone V print* with the normal contrast *Zone VI* print. If an approximate match is obtained, an N+1 development time has been found.

Now observe the upper zones. Depending on the developer used, an N+1 development at Zone V may produce an N+1½ to N+2 at Zone VII or VIII. For example, what was exposed for Zone VII may, after the N+1 development, print in Zone VIII or even in IX.

The N+1 development situation may be remedied a little by the use of diluted developers. It is possible to have the N+1 Zone V (into VI) without losing the Zone VIII into Zone X. Diluted developers make it possible to increase slightly the density of the moderately exposed middle tones before the upper zone densities are developed beyond printable limits. These changes are slight but at times worth doing. Whatever the reason for this action, diluted developers, in most cases, slow down the rate of development on the highly exposed areas of the negative most, and on the slightly exposed areas least, and allow moderately exposed areas to be raised somewhat before upper zone densities are developed beyond printable limits.

### N+2 Calibrations

To find a starting point for determining an N+2 development time, increase your N+1 development time by whatever factor produced your N+1 expansion. For example, if a 30% increase (Normal development time x 1.3) gave you an N+1, take the N+1 time and increase it 30% (N+1 development time x 1.3). For N+2 compare the Zone V exposure to Zone VII.

**When the expansion calibrations are completed, field test expansions with care—and frequently.**

*Adams believes that with continuous development, a dilute developer would —with longer time—give the same contrast as a more concentrated developer. It is when the interval between agitation is increased that the "exhaustion" effect takes over and the high density areas are less affected than the low density areas.*

## Two Problems

Two examples follow that compare two developers, each used to its best advantage. After reading, find subjects that fit the situations described and photograph according to the plan given.

### Dilution 1:3 or 1:4

**The Scene:**    After placing an important shadow value on Zone III, a *significant* subject value, skin for example, falls on Zone V, and an upper high value, a white curtain somewhere, falls on Zone VII.

**The Problem:**    To raise the skin tone to Zone VI without pushing the upper high value beyond Zone VIII where it would become a textureless white print value.

**The Solution:**    An N+1 expansion with a developer such as D-76 or D-23, diluted 1:3 or 1:4. Intermittent agitation is very important here.

### Straight Developer

**The Scene:**    After placing an important subject shadow value on Zone III, the only highlight value falls on Zone V; the scene is flat with little separation between subject values.

**The Problem:**    To raise the high value at least two zones without bringing up the lower values, in order to maximize the separation in tone between subject values.

**The Solution:**    An N+2 expansion with straight developer such as D-76, D-23, or HC-110 stock 1:3 (a high contrast dilution).

This suggests a new series of calibrations. If undertaken, the standard calibration series can be adapted to various dilutions and developers, for example, Acufine, D-23 at 1:1, 1:2, 1:3, etc. In fact the ardent technician can lose himself or herself in testing dilutions.

*Field-test expansions as soon as these calibrations are completed. Explore expansion for the sake of compensating. Why do it? Investigate how expansion affects local contrast. What is the sensation, the feeling of expansion, the body knowledge of it?*

## Compaction Calibrations

### N−1

To find a starting point for an N−1 compaction, decrease your Normal development time 30% for high speed films (ASA 400), 20% for medium speed films (ASA 125), and 15% for low speed films (ASA 32-50).

1. Expose your standard textured subject to Zones I through X at your calibrated (adjusted) exposure index. Develop the negatives at the estimated N−1 development time. Print all the negatives on normal contrast paper at the standard print time.
2. Compare the N−1 prints with your calibrated normal contrast prints by laying both sets out as parallel zone rulers. First compare Zones I through III: they may be a little darker. If so, it is because film speed *decreases* when the development time is reduced.
3. Finally, compare the compacted Zone VIII print with the normal contrast Zone VII print. If an approximate match is obtained, an N−1 development time has been found. Observe the changes between the two rulers for all the Zones.

### N−2 and N−3

To find a starting point for determining N−2 development times, decrease your N−1 time by the same factor which produced your N−1 time. Development times less than three minutes or less than ½-Normal are **not recommended.**

### General Considerations about Compactions

Development times of three minutes or less (whether they are ½-Normal development time or not) are difficult to work with. The likelihood of uneven development increases. Hence a one-minute presoak in water, followed by continuous agitation in the developer is recommended for short development times. If a greater degree of compaction is desired than you can accomplish in three minutes, change to the next higher dilution. For example if working with 1:1 the next dilution is 1:2 (D-76 type developer).

We find that, in general, compactions with developers used either full-strength or diluted 1:1 maintain film speed; higher dilutions lose film speed and thus are less desirable. The compensating developers D-76 and D-23 are examples of developers which function well as either full-strength or 1:1 compaction developers. Kodak HC-110 and Edwal FG7, on the other hand, are examples of highly concentrated developers that are designed to be used diluted for all types of development. For example the FG7 concentrate can be diluted 1:7 for N−1, and 1:15 for N−2 compactions, so as to avoid extremely short development times.

Compaction development by the two-solution and water-bath methods can no longer be recommended for modern thin-emulsion films, because they do not absorb sufficient developer solution to continue developing in the second bath.

## Contrast-Control in Excess of N+2 and N−2

Modern films do not respond well to over or underdevelopment. The range from N+2 to N−2 represents the practical limits of film development changes. (That is optimistic.) Less development than N−2 results in poor separation and a substantial loss of effective film speed; more than N+2 development results in an increase of graininess and fog level, particularly with roll film. However, as Ansel Adams points out, negative grain from long development can actually improve the sense of texture and definition in low-contrast highly-textured subjects.*

Consequently when the subject contrast range calls for an expansion or compaction greater than N+2 of N−2, *paper contrast grades are combined with variable film development.* For example, an N+2 development printed on an N+2 (#5) paper = N+4 (almost).

Beyond the N+4 and N−4 controls we resort to special techniques: "fill-in" lights, or flash fill, and pre-exposure to reduce contrast; inherently high contrast film and filters to increase contrast.

*Ansel Adams, "The Zone System for 35mm Photography," **The Leica Manual,** 15th Edition, Morgan & Morgan, p 233.*

*Combine paper grade control with film development control, for example:*

*N+1 paper contrast*
*+N+1 film development*
*=N+2 contrast-control*

**Pre-exposure**

**1.** Film in camera is exposed to a textureless surface or area, sky or gray card for example.

**2.** Expose for Zone I, or II at the most.

**3.** Contrast of subject is then calculated as one, or two, zones (stops) less than the meter indicates (one if you pre-exposed for Zone I, two if for Zone II).

**4.** Proceed to expose photograph assuming that texture will appear in the Zone II areas as if it were Zone III.

**5.** The upper end of the scale will be unaffected.

The reason why the upper zones will be unaffected appears obvious in a simple table of *zones* related to *exposure units*.

| | I | II | III | IV | V | VI | VII | VIII | IX | zones |
|---|---|---|---|---|---|---|---|---|---|---|
| | 1 | 2 | 4 | 8 | 16 | 32 | 64 | 128 | 256 | units of exposure |
| Add | 1 | 1 | 1 | 1 | 1 | 1 | 1 | 1 | 1 | unit of pre-exposure |
| | 2 | 3 | 5 | 9 | 17 | 33 | 65 | 129 | 257 | |

This technique of pre-exposure can rarely be taken beyond two zones because the low values begin to fog over. The method works well in combination with compactions.

*A special technique used for "reducing" contrast of subjects. It is one of several mentioned on the previous page.*

## Development and Exposure Compensations

**Plus and Minus Development Require Exposure Compensations To Keep Zone I in Place.**
At the outset of zone system study we assume that variable development (time and dilution) affects the upper zones most and the lower zones least. After calibrating a few films we know that "least" includes slight changes in Zones I, II and III. These slight changes in density can be understood as film speed changes. The following table offers starting points for investigating this phenomenon.

| Development Symbol | Approximate Exposure Compensation |
|---|---|
| N+2 | 1 stop decrease |
| N+1 | ½ stop decrease |
| N−1 | ½ stop increase |
| N−2 | 1 stop increase |

Because of paper exposure scale limitations, even Normal film developments are about 60% compacted from an ideal development. Consequently, further reduced development lowers film speed, resulting in a loss of shadow detail. By comparison, expansion compensations are more desirable because shadow detail is enhanced. Photographers can empirically take advantage of the compensation table above whenever the situation arises. Yet there is more to this exposure-development interaction, as we will see at the end of this chapter.

## Summary of Film and Paper Contrast Control

### A. Film Contrast Control

| Subject Range in Zones | Development Symbol | |
|---|---|---|
| 8 | N+2 | |
| 9 | N+1 | |
| 10 | N | Rendered full-scale |
| 11 | N−1 | 10 zones |
| 12 | N−2 | |

### B. Paper Contrast Control (assumes N film development)

| Subject Range in Zones | Contrast Symbol | Paper Grades | |
|---|---|---|---|
| 8½ | N+2 | #5-6 | |
| 9 | N+1 | #4-5 | |
| 10 | N | #2-3 | Rendered full-scale |
| 11 | N−1 | #1-2 | 10 zones |
| 11½ | N−2 | #0-1 | |

### C. Combined Contrast Controls

| Film Development Symbol | Paper Grade | Total Contrast Control | Print Rendering of Subject |
|---|---|---|---|
| N+2 | #5 | N+4 | 6-zone subject rendered |
| N+1 | #4 | N+3 | full scale |
| N | #3 or #2 | | |
| N−1 | #1 | N−2 | |
| N−2 | #1 | N−3 | 13-zone subject rendered full scale |

For N+1 or N−1 a choice is open. Either change film development or paper grade. The quality difference is subtle, but real. The photographer should explore this fact for himself.

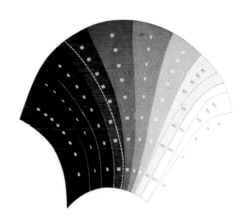

**Zone Systemizer's Gray Scale**

We would like to draw the reader's attention to the Zone Systemizer (Morgan and Morgan). This consists of a special exposure-development calculator dial, devised by John Dowdell. The feature significant at the moment is its gray scale. In use, it can be read for the amount of exposure required to compensate for various expansions and compactions.

# Alternative Planning Routines

The reader may have gotten the false impression that contrast-control consists of two meter readings, high and low. That, of course, is the simplest way of measuring contrast. The middle values, however, need to be taken into account. Sometimes middle values determine placement, no question about that. Two different samples follow: both begin the planning with a middle value placement, that is, in Zones IV, V, or VI. One is known as a "three-reading-routine", and the other, its author calls "bi-directional contrast-control."

## Three-tone-reading routine

The following model will suggest how to develop a "three-tone-reading" routine when certain middle values are critically important to the photograph. Zone system shorthand notations should be readable by now.

Light Value Readings: Low 6; high 13; critical value 10, and designated for Zone VI. Look at the situation on a zone ruler.

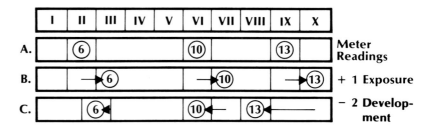

**A.** Light Value Readings

**B.** Plus one (+1) exposure moves each value equally one zone up the scale.

**C.** Minus two (−2) development moves each value unequally down the scale. The higher values are shifted most.

To get the critical value, 10, in Zone VI, the low value will fall in Zone II, which is too low to render shadow area detail. And this makes the high value fall in Zone IX, too high for texture. A two-step procedure, B and C, is the solution.

Becoming aware of local contrasts in the middle tones seems to be the next step in achieving a well-crafted approach to the art of photography.

## An Alternative Mode For Visual Thinking

Interface, visual thinking, shaping/discovery go on during calibrating as well as photographing. Discoveries have been made in that realm as well. Lorenz presents such a finding. It is an alternative mode to the already familiar, "Expose for Zone III and develop to Zone VII." The alternative reads, "Expose for Zone V and develop for Zone I and VII.

Its main feature is formulated thus: by exposing film (sheet or roll) one stop less than normal (N−1 exposure) and developing it to the equivalent of one stop more than normal (N+1 development), a metered Zone V exposure will continue to yield a middle gray print value. Above and below Zone V, however, the contrast will change. As table A below indicates, N+ exposure can be combined with N− development to lower contrast, while N− exposure combined with N+ development increases contrast on both sides of a "stationary" Zone V.

### Table A

| Exposure Changes | Development Changes | Rendering of Zone V | Contrast Effect |
|---|---|---|---|
| N+2 | N−2 | Middle Gray | Lowest |
| N+1 | N−1 | "     " | Lower |
| N | N | "     " | Normal |
| N−1 | N+1 | "     " | Higher |
| N−2 | N+2 | "     " | Highest |

This alternative approach is an extension of our remembering to compensate exposure for variable development. (More exposure is needed with N− development and less exposure with N+ development to keep Zones I-III in place.) The alternative method goes a step further by increasing or decreasing exposure measured in zones enough to keep Zone V in place with both N− and N+ developments, also measured in zones. With that discovery a different way of thinking emerged. Whereas we usually vary

**Schematic for Bi-directional Contrast-Control.**

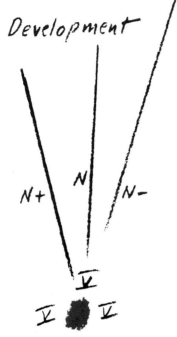

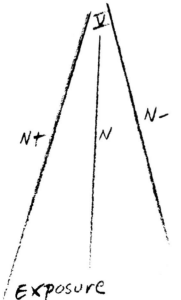

development to affect the upper end of the scale vigorously while holding the lower end constant, now we can hold the middle (Zone V) constant and let both ends of the scale change contrast. Lows are made darker as abruptly as highs made lighter when we combined N− exposure with N+ development. Conversely, lows are made darker as gradually as highs made lighter when we combine N+ exposure with N− development.

That was the first noticeable effect; it leads to a second: Each combination of exposure and development yields a different exposure scale, from as few as five to as many as eleven zones. Ultimately, five scales were obtained: the normal contrast scale, and two scales each of less and greater than normal contrast, as indicated in Table B.

**Table B**

| Exposure | Development | Exposure Scale | Contrast Effect |
|---|---|---|---|
| N+2 | N−2 | 11 zones | Lowest |
| N+1 | N−1 | 10 zones | Lower |
| N | N | 9 zones | Normal |
| N−1 | N+1 | 7 zones | Higher |
| N−2 | N+2 | 5 zones | Highest |

That observation subtly altered our visual thinking again. If development N+1 together with exposure N−1 produced a seven-zone scale, and so on, those scales could be compared to 8 tone or 12 tone musical scales. We could play the same normal print on five different octaves! As our thinking became more abstract, we could see producing different scales by predetermined manipulation.

Finally, a third effect was discovered which rounded out the concept. If the exposure index calculator on the luminance meter were used instead of F-stops to change exposure, the meter's indicated exposure would continue to read and subsequently render Zone V as a middle gray print value, regardless of which scale was being used. Such adjustment would then permit the meter to be calibrated not only to the normal exposure scale, but to the N− and N+ scales as well.*

*The range of exposure zones rendered as print values between black and white on normal contrast paper.

84

Table C summarizes the effect of using the exposure index to vary exposure for a film rated at exposure index 200 for the normal contrast scale.

**Table C**

| Exposure Change | Meter Calculator** Exposure Index | Development Change | Scale |
|---|---|---|---|
| N+2 | 50 | N−2 | 11 Zones |
| N+1 | 100 | N−1 | 10 |
| N | 200 | N | 9 |
| N−1 | 400 | N+1 | 7 |
| N−2 | 800 | N+2 | 5 |

For example, if after metering the brightness range of the scene you choose the 10 zone, lower-than-normal contrast scale, set the exposure index calculator on your meter to 100 and expose in your usual way. Develop this sheet or roll later to N−1 to keep Zone V in place on both meter and print.

Thus the visual thinking about scales as a "package" was completed. Lorenz refers to it as "bi-directional contrast control."

Diagram A corresponds to how we might visually think about this effect. The visualizing mind grasps it quite easily. However we know better: we know that black and white terminate the scales of all photographic papers. So it is the number of zones between that change.

Because black and white are included, Diagram A visually fits the facts better than the schematic on the opposite page. Inversely changing exposure and development indexes causes the zones to widen under the influence of expanded developments as we move from scale to scale; and to narrow under the influence of compactions.

Five scales are compared in detail by Diagram B, next page. They are quite abstract, and originate in tests on Ilford FP4 film using the same methods of exposing a textured object as in the calculated series presented in Chapter 2. The specific data is gathered in the adjacent table.

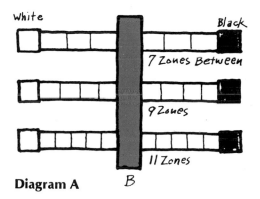

**Diagram A**       B

*Sketch for Bi-directional Contrast-Control.*

**Though we alter the exposure index, the actual film speed remains the same.

85

**Compactions**

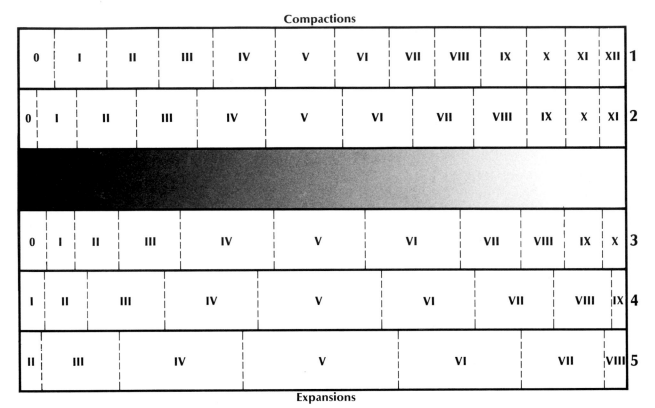

**Expansions**

**Diagram B**

|  | Development | Exposure | Scale in Zones Between B&W |
|---|---|---|---|
| Scale 1 | N−2 | N+2 | 11 |
| Scale 2 | N−1 | N+1 | 10 |
| Scale 3 | N | N | 9 |
| Scale 4 | N+1 | N−1 | 7 |
| Scale 5 | N+2 | N−2 | 5 |

As exposure is decreased and development increased, the print value interval for middle zone exposures begins to widen. Maximum separation in print values between adjacent subject brightnesses is achieved. More exposure and less development produces the opposite result. Adjacent subject brightnesses are rendered with less separation in tone.

If one stop more exposure is coupled with an N-1 development, a 1/2-zone loss in effective film speed from the reduced development will result in only a 1/2-zone net increase in Zone I.

If two stops more exposure is coupled with an N-2 development, a one-zone loss in effective film speed from the reduced development will result in a one-zone increase in Zone I.

## Sample of Simultaneous Exposure/Development Changes

**Film: Ilford FP4***

| Adjusted Exposure Index | Development Symbol | Developer (D-76) Dilution | Time at 68°F | Average Gradient |
|---|---|---|---|---|
| 16 (25%, or ¼-normal) | N−2 | 1:1 | 4½ min. Agitation Plan I | 0.40 |
| 32 (50%, or ½-normal) | N−1 | 1:1 | 6 min. Agitation Plan II | 0.45 |
| 64 (Normal Index) | N | 1:3 | 11 min. Agitation Plan III | 0.50 |
| 125 (2x normal) | N+1 | 1:2 | 9½ min. Agitation Plan III | 0.65 |
| 320 (6x normal) | N+2½ | Straight | 11½ min. Agitation Plan III | 0.85 |

* Exposure to a textured target subject was set at Zone V in all instances. Flare was kept at a minimum by working in a dark-walled room.

Ordinarily meters in the zone system are calibrated to the Normal scale only. By manipulating the exposure index on the meter, in effect, we can "calibrate" four other scales: N+2, N+2, N+1, N−2. Consequently we can visualize directly from the face of the meter for the plus and minus scales just as we are accustomed to read Normal. Heretofore, in order to visualize the effects of a possible compaction or expansion, we thought of scales that fluctuate widely at the upper end and barely at all at the lower end. (Sometimes we got an image of a dog wagging its tail.) The visualization pattern associated with this thought may be sketched as shown on the next page.

*Visualization pattern for customary zone system thinking about compactions and expansions.*

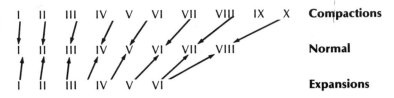

A sketch of the "Bi-directional" alternative shows a significantly different sketch for visualization.

*Visualization pattern for "Bi-directional" compactions and expansions.*

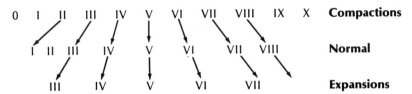

Taking Zone V as a pivot for visualizing and photographing, instead of Zones III and VII, puts a different light on practice. Instead of planning more or less development to reach a norm, we can think of fitting a subject scale with an appropriate print scale. If the subject has 11 zones, we match it with an 11-zone scale (N−2 development plus N+2 exposure).

When we extend these diagrams, abstract as they are, to field work, five scales take on visual identities complete with feelings that the imagination can grasp. In due time an abstract seven-zone scale, for instance, acquires a certain flavor quite unlike the taste of an 11-zone scale. A seven-zone scale tastes like expansion and all that mode implies to our feelings. An 11- or 12-zone scale arouses feelings and sensations associated with compactions.

Enough data lies buried in the paragraphs above to get a photographer experimenting with this alternative "three reading" mode. Sampling both modes, probably expecting to choose one or the other for keeps, is fine. But we suggest making both alternatives so familiar that switching from one to the other becomes second nature, and therefore another means of keeping in touch with constantly changing visual situations. Any learned ability to "switch scales" would help the photographer-reader to deal with the shaping/discovery problems of camerawork.

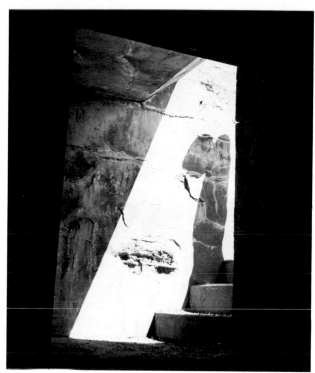

Peter Lorenz

**A. An Over Scaled Subject. . .**

**B. Rendered as a Full Substance Photograph.**

*The scene brightness range was 9 zones from the important shadow to the important brights. I wanted the entryway shadows to be rendered middle gray, without losing the foreground to black or wall in sun to white.*

*My meter readings indicated that if the shadows on the far wall were placed in Zone V, the foreground would fall between Zones I and II, while the wall in sunlight would fall in Zones IX and X. I chose the lowest*

*bi-directional scale (N+2 exposure, N−2 development) to simultaneously raise the shadows and lower the brights, while maintaining a placed subject value in Zone V. I have tried to show, as far as the printed page will permit, the subtle difference between an over-scaled rendering and a full-substance (detail everywhere) photograph. In both prints the shadows on the entryway wall remain within Zone V, even though that area in Print A is a little darker than Print B.*

89

Anna Rose Morton, **Gijon, Spain, 1974**
Pin-hole photograph by Jim Haberman

90

# The Print As a Performance of the Negative

The reader-photographer who has completed her or his first set of calibrations may feel at the beginning of something new: growth ahead, predicting tonalities successfully, being in control of contrast, etc. If this book were a flesh and blood teacher, at this moment he would encourage the reader to find the freedom hidden in the new knowledge. He would wait patiently until the reader returned weeks or months later with prints to show, and with questions that grew out of experience. During their talk together, the points about to be made would arise naturally. But this is a book, and thus timing is thrown to the gods. Which means that you should read, work, think and read again.

During calibration, the reader doubtlessly observed that only care and precision assured reliable results; so she or he learned to be careful and accurate. Improving craftsmanship by attention to precision can only be to the good, and so it is—up to a point. Beyond that meaningless standards of accuracy set in, which in practice are unattainable and unnecessary. A latitude of approximately one zone covers normal equipment tolerances and a few human slips. Previsualization, we repeat, also benefits by a one-zone tolerance. In the darkroom we expect that, having been careful, the standard print exposure time will yield a work print with everything rendered in the zones planned. Then we fine-tune with small exposure changes, different developers, and so on, to shape a fine print. At times we are rewarded with a fine photograph at the first exposure, but what an exception that is—in fact it feels like an accident!

If we devise and abide by some such discipline for ourselves, we open ourselves to see more deeply at the inception of the next photograph. How? By reducing darkroom manipulation to minimum fine-tuning. So we must direct extraordinary attention to the subject before exposure. We must see it more intently, scrutinize with the intention of "feeling" our way into it. We need to experience the scene with emotions as well as body, make technical and aesthetic judgements based on "feeling into." Seeing and planning: together they become the creative craft. That would be craft as potters, weavers or furniture makers understand it — union with product in the midst of the process.

Against an exclusively disciplined non-interpretative, tone-for-tone attitude toward the negative, we would like to stand the concept of the negative as a score, and the print as a record of a performance of that score, if not *the* performance.

This attitude suggests a succession of proofs and work prints that may lead to a final interpretation other than planned. Take any negative, yours or a friend's and, without reference to original intentions, follow the negative to its visual conclusions. So doing amounts to an exploration of the negative comparable to exploring a scene-subject by previsualization. Exploring negatives with prints soon leads to an ability to previsualize options from negatives before any print is made.

Occasionally we find negatives that yield two or three equally vital interpretations, distinct "image statements" with differences well beyond subtle variations. An advanced performer's relation to a negative, whether acquainted with this system or not, may be compared to musicians who change their occasionally interpretation of a score. Their critics take note and their listeners make comment on the differences. The same could apply to photographers' various printings. As we have found, some negatives contain vital variants. The photographer can elect to find the one most significant rendering (interpretation) of a negative, however long it takes. On the other hand he may elect to print the negative according to his mood, whatever that may be, whenever he reprints (plays) it. Musicians are expected to take time to understand a score; experienced photographers report that the same is required of them by their negatives. Occasionally, a negative will keep pace with one's inner growth for several years. Comparing a rendering made ten years ago to a current print, the photographer frequently is seen to have been in two different places. Whether one is "ahead" of the other is hard to say, but they certainly do differ.

*The craft problem may be approached as soon as one film is completely calibrated: adjusted exposure index, normal development, plus and minus developments.*

*Get acquainted with this idea by planning and executing various options with several subjects.*

*Negatives which seem to keep up with inner growth are characteristically full of printable detail in all their parts. (This is true of "useful" negatives for all kinds of purposes.) When all ten zones are present and alive, one can suppress locally, or increase contrast locally, print with all zones fully visible, or merge some with one another. By comparison, negatives made to produce a specific kind of print are less likely to be responsive to the contrast controls available—but not invariably. We must note in closing that subject matter itself, the unique disposition of tones and zones, plays as large a part in the final photograph as tonal control alone. These matters, however, are topics of the Visualization Manual.*

*Somehow negatives acquire "personalities"—co-operative, resistant, downright antagonistic, adamant in keeping their secret to themselves. In one way or another most negatives, including systemized ones, are "reluctant dragons"*

# The Graphs of Sensitometry

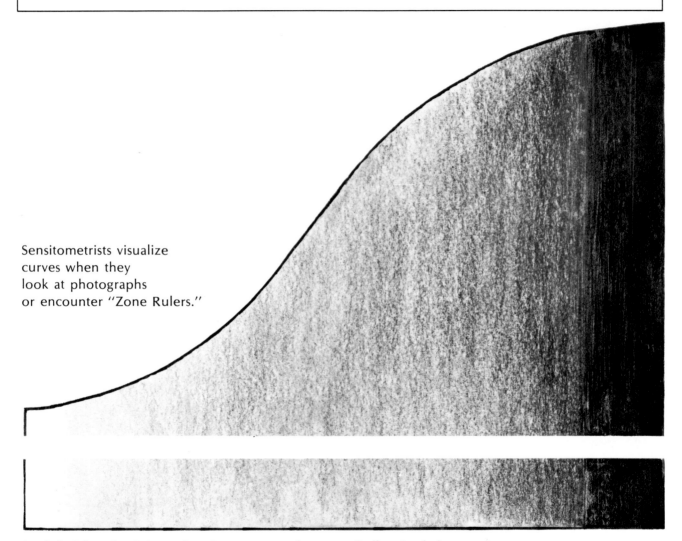

Sensitometrists visualize
curves when they
look at photographs
or encounter "Zone Rulers."

**Symbol of the D-log E curve of sensitometry seen above a vertically extended zone ruler.**

*Sensitometrists learn to mentally visualize their special kind of curves whenever they see photographs. Photographers who learn to emulate sensitometric "see-* *ing," develop a clearer inner vision of how his materials affect his "seeing."*

## The Sensitometrist Speaks

**W**hen I look at a D-log E curve, I can see and almost feel the living relationships between subject values and zones, between exposure zones and negative densities, between print exposures and tonal values in the print. Finally the curve is an equivalent for the photographer's visualization from subject to print.

As I write the word equivalent, I am reminded of the sun and cloud photographs Alfred Stieglitz made in the 1920's to be equivalents of his thoughts and feelings. I feel much the same way among sensitometric graphs. Looking at a certain curve, by virtue of the densities in film or print it is equivalent to, I can experience texture, contrast, accent, substance, and other subtleties. It took me a long time, by myself, to learn this. Perhaps that is why I would like to help you do the same, but sooner. Please be assured that the graphs of sensitometry will add another dimension to your visualization, another comprehension of your calibrations, past and future.

Different levels of photography require different levels of understanding and skill. A "press the button, let George do the rest" photographer needs little or no technical knowledge of photography. A zone system photographer takes more responsibility. He visualizes before he presses the button, and afterwards calibrates for predictable print values.

Through the abstractions and equivalents left us by Hurter and Driffield, the beauty of the zone system can be re-experienced, not as calibrations nor previsualization, although these are included, but as science. Sensitometry offers a third view of photography pertinent to responsibility.

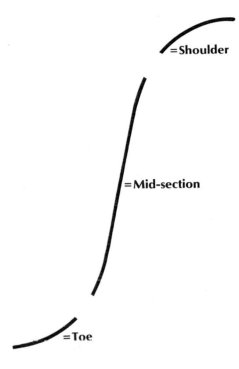

*The D-log E curve:*
*An equivalent of the effect of light and chemistry on silver halides dispersed in thin layers*

**A D-log E curve has three sections**

**From the slope of the mid-section I read contrast and "sense" texture**

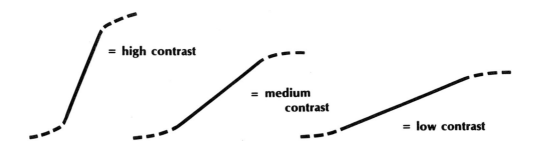

= high contrast

= medium contrast

= low contrast

*It is in the mid-section that doubling the exposure produces the largest density change in the negative or print, consequently texture is well rendered.*

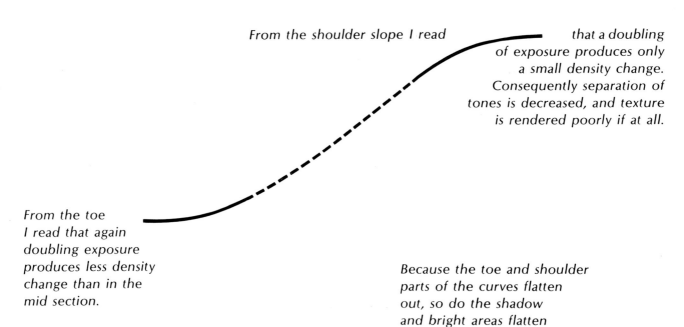

*From the shoulder slope I read*

*that a doubling of exposure produces only a small density change. Consequently separation of tones is decreased, and texture is rendered poorly if at all.*

*From the toe I read that again doubling exposure produces less density change than in the mid section.*

*Because the toe and shoulder parts of the curves flatten out, so do the shadow and bright areas flatten in the print.*

*From the grid of sensitometric graphs*

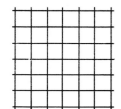

I
read
density
along
the
side

D ————————
e ————————
n ————————
s ————————
i ————————
t ————————
y ————————

E x p o s u r e
*and exposure along the bottom*

When numbers appear they are logarithms. This is done, in part, so that the graphs will fit on the page. If numbered arithmetically, the page would have to be several feet square.

D 1.8 ————————
e 1.5 ————————
n 1.2 ————————
s 0.9
i 0.6 ————————
t 0.3 ————————
y 0.0 ————————

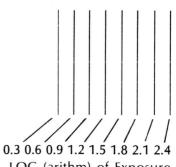

0.3 0.6 0.9 1.2 1.5 1.8 2.1 2.4
LOG (arithm) of Exposure

The two, density and log of exposure are abbreviated: **D-log E.** Since density is a logarithm, both density and log exposure can be expressed as zones.

D ———————— VII
e ———————— VI
n ———————— V
s ———————— IV
i ———————— III
t ———————— II
y ———————— I

I  II  III IV V VI VII VIII
E x p o s u r e

Our experiences with zone rulers and calibration verify that from III into VII are fully textured zones; and that the zones on either end are poorly textured or not at all. When I draw a D-log E curve on a grid, I can see why—the contrast is less at either end than in the mid-section.

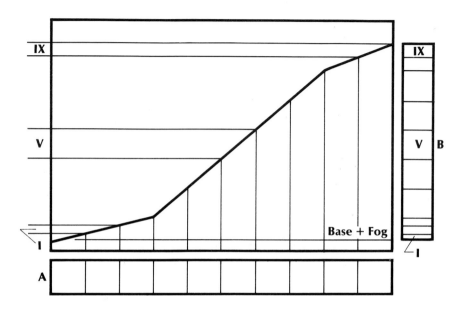

**Corresponding Exposure Zones**
*Notice that although subject values (exposures) (A) increase by one-stop increments, print values (densities) do not (B).*

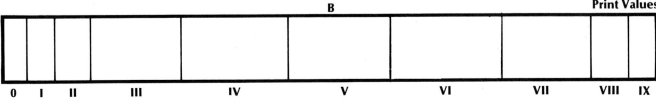

| | | | | A | | | | | Subject Values |
|---|---|---|---|---|---|---|---|---|---|
| 0 | I | II | III | IV | V | VI | VII | VIII | IX |

**D-log E curves reveal a new form for the familiar zone ruler**

Print Values

| | | | | | B | | | | | |
|---|---|---|---|---|---|---|---|---|---|---|

0  I  II  III  IV  V  VI  VII  VIII  IX

*With a new print value scale,
Visualization may be refined.*

After an "overture", the remainder of this section is divided into three movements reminiscent of music: Photograph, Negative, and Zone (Tone) Reproduction. Throughout the three movements we will continue to study scales, but from another viewpoint. What else but the D-log E curve could be the common denominator for exposure scales, negative density scales, subject value scales, and print value scales (zone rulers)? We find that each type of paper and film has its own "personality" which visualization must either conform to or use expressively. In the Zone Reproduction cycle, each subject value is traced from scene to negative to print. But there the cycle stops because sensitometry assumes that other disciplines will investigate the effect of values and zones on the viewer of photographs. The section ends with the "proceed with caution" coda.

Progressing through these "movements," sensitometrists and photographers alike need to keep in mind that while the zone system photographer manipulates the process to produce what he wants out of the whole spectrum of "prints with feeling," the sensitometrist is primarily concerned with fidelity of reproduction. The three authors working together noticed that picture-minded photographers tend to twist D-log E curves into their own form of visual poetics. Thus the one system data pertain to free interpretation, while the sensitometric data are based on a literal interpretations of scenes and subjects.

*Sensitometric data are based on a literal interpretation of the scene. Using the same data in zone system terms encourages free interpretation.*

# Terminology

**Density:** A measure of the amount of light absorbed by a negative, transparency or print.

**Logarithm:** Shorthand for scaling large numbers. Zones are a visual shorthand for a certain set of logarithms, the type known as "to the base 2". So are shutter speeds, f-stops, light value scales on luminance meters. We are familiar with the geometric progression of:

| Shutter speeds | 1 | 1/2 | 1/4 | 1/8 | 1/16 | etc. |
|---|---|---|---|---|---|---|
| f-stops | 5.6 | 8 | 11 | 16 | 22 | etc. |
| Zones | I | II | III | IV | V | etc. |
| Light Values | 1 | 2 | 3 | 4 | 5 | etc. |

They can all be expressed as logarithms to the base 2.

The density of negatives and prints, however, is expressed in logs to the base 10. A neat relationship of interest to photographers exists between these two bases. Each base-2 step relates to three base-10 steps thus:

| $\log_{10}$ steps | 0.0 | 0.1 | 0.2 | 0.3 | 0.4 | 0.5 | 0.6 | 0.7 | 0.8 | 0.9 | etc. |
|---|---|---|---|---|---|---|---|---|---|---|---|
| $\log_2$ steps | 1 | | | 2 | | | 3 | | | 4 | etc. |

The same neat relationship extends to zones and densities.

**D-log E curve:** D = density, log = logarithm, E = exposure. This curve on a graph describes the relationships between exposure, development, and density. (Also called, "characteristic curve," and "H & D curve," after Hurter and Driffield. Recently "H" is being used for exposure, hence it is sometimes seen as "D-log H.")

**Zone (Tone) Reproduction:** Visual relationships traced in zones between scene luminances, negative densities, and print values. Sensitometry names this Tone Reproduction.

**Gradient and Contrast Index:** The slope in the mid-section of D-log E curves is named Gradient; and the development-contrast derived from the angle is named Contrast Index. A 45° angle from the horizontal is assigned the number 1.0. Speaking zonally, 1.0 gradient means that a zone "input of light" to film, yields a "zone of output" as seen in the photograph (or negative). A 45° angle signifies input = output. Contrary to expectations the gradient for Normal film development is 0.6. This means that output is only 60% of input. Nevertheless because of the paper scale, approximately 0.6 is "average development" for most films.
(See Appendix B)

**Speed Point:** One of various means for deriving a film speed rating for exposure. Currently, a film density 0.1 above base-plus-fog is taken as speed point (Zone I). Step One of Calibration is to establish a speed index based on the Zone I negative.

# Photographic and Paper Characteristics

Characteristic D-log E curves are abstractions and, as in looking at abstractions in art, it may be difficult at first to visualize pictures from them. But once understood, the relations between exposure and measurable density reveal a simple and harmonious relationship basic to visualization. If the curve is imagined as a ski slope, it becomes apparent that most of the action occurs in the mid-section. An analogous behavior occurs in film and photographs; the mid-section of any curve has the steepest slope, the most contrast, the most texture. Since the local contrast in the toe and the shoulder is relatively flat, textures disappear.

Textures disappear at specific points on the curve. It is convenient to know numerically where the "cut-off points" in a print are: .04 density for high value texture (toe) and about 1.7 for shadow detail (shoulder).

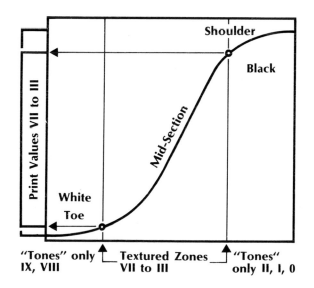

A. Paper Curve: Three Sections
Texture Cut-off Points indicated at toe and shoulder

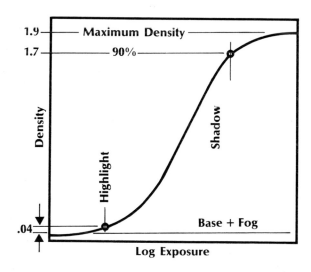

B. Paper Curve: Cut-off Points
Actual densities are indicated

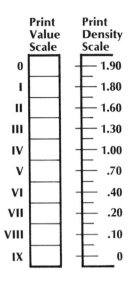

| Print Value Scale | Print Density Scale |
|---|---|
| 0 | 1.90 |
| I | 1.80 |
| II | 1.60 |
| III | 1.30 |
| IV | 1.00 |
| V | .70 |
| VI | .40 |
| VII | .20 |
| VIII | .10 |
| IX | 0 |

*Print values are equivalent
To print densities*

*Each Print Value represents a cluster of values (zones). Note that the density scale is distorted to coincide with an idealized Print Value scale. (Be cautioned that the actual density numbers will vary depending on the various papers used. A density of 0.70 is about an 18% gray and is used as a pivot point.)*

*In this table the changes in exposure (speed) are relative to Grade #2 printed for 16 seconds.*

*The data are for example only: This manufacturer's product include approximately a three-stop difference from paper Grade 0 to Grade 5. Other brands may be more or less.*

Cut-off points noted, textured-only and tonal-only sections observed, let's see the sensitometric view of paper grades, paper contrast, and paper speed.

The family of curves on the adjoining page belongs to 6 grades of a paper from a certain manufacturer. The *grades* are numbered in the familiar 0 through 5. The *contrasts* are differentiated by the steepness of the slope, 0 being the least contrasty and 5 the most. Interestingly enough, the sensitometrist looking at this family of curves sees progression, even "movement." As the paper grade *advances* from 0 to 5, the slope of the curve gets steeper, and therefore the contrast of the paper increases.

The *speed* of the various grades is noted thus: As the curve *shifts* to the left it is the speed that increases. That is, 0 paper is faster than 5. It requires less exposure.

The horizontal *exposure axis* at 0.6 (Zone V) density is the "line" the speed increases on, moving left: moving right on it, the contrast increases. So this axis must be important. It is. A print density of 0.6 is taken as the "speed point" for paper. Thus a horizontal line moving from 0.60 and intersecting all of the curves, indicates the change in exposure necessary to obtain a density of 0.60 for each of the different paper grades. To get the data from the graph to the enlarging easel requires a certain ritual. Dotted lines are dropped from the exposure axis to the Log E (exposure) axis below. Then, since each 0.30 Log E increment represents 1 stop difference in exposure, the various speeds can be differentiated in stops. A sample table shows this.

| Paper Grade | Exposure change in stops | Speed, Relative to Grade .2 |
|---|---|---|
| 0 | − 1-2/3 stops | 5 seconds |
| 1 | − 2/3 " | 10 " |
| 2 | — | 16 " |
| 3 | + 2/3 " | 25 " |
| 4 | + 1-1/3 " | 40 " |
| 5 | + 1-1/2 " | 45 " |

The sensitometrist looking at these curves, sees and speaks of progression and "movement" left to right, and back. If the reader can grasp the sense of this "movement", he or she will begin to get a sense of a three-dimensional graph. When graphs and curves are sensed in this manner, visualization has something new at its command.

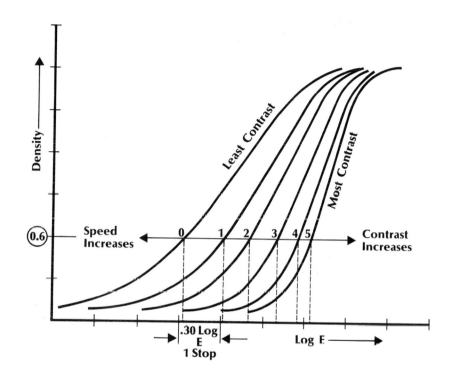

Resin Coated (RC) papers behave in the same way generally. They have specific characteristics slightly different of course. The greatest change is in the fixing washing and drying phases.

## Paper Grade: Contrast and Speed
A family of curves for different grades of paper from one manufacturer. As the slope of the curve steepens, the contrast of the paper increases. The less the exposure required to get a density of 0.6 (Zone V) above base + fog, the faster is the paper speed. This "movement" is measured along the horizontal line at Density 0.60.

## Paper Exposure Range

How do different paper grades accommodate negative density ranges that vary from flat to contrasty?

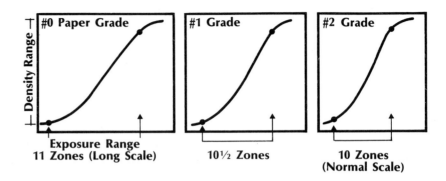

Exposure Range
**11 Zones (Long Scale)**      **10½ Zones**      **10 Zones (Normal Scale)**

*The blacks and whites remain unchanged. It is the number of zones between that change.*
*As paper grade number increases, exposure range decreases.*

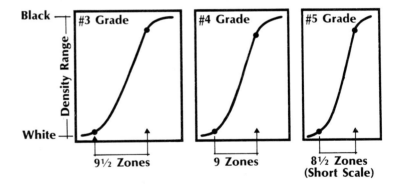

**9½ Zones**      **9 Zones**      **8½ Zones (Short Scale)**

Here the family of paper curves on the previous page, are separated for better visibility. Observe that while the slope increases from Grade 0 to 5, *the black to white contrast range (the Density Range) remains fixed.* Thinking zonally, blackness and whiteness do *not* change from grade to grade, but the *number of zones* between does. (This is true only if all the grades being compared have the same surface; either glossy or matte. Because glossy-surface papers reach maximum density at about 1.90 their blacks are darker than matte papers, which reach maximum density at about 1.60.)

## Paper Exposure Range and Negative Contrast

In the first chapter, we saw certain photographs that illustrated the effect of printing short-scale negatives on long-scale papers and the reverse. Here is another way to look at the same options.

Three terms are important: overscaled, full-scaled, and underscaled. Full-scaled means that negative and paper scales match. Underscaled means that the negative scale is shorter than the paper exposure range (scale); consequently some tones are missing in the photograph. Overscaled means that the negative contrast range (scale) is longer than the paper exposure range, hence some tones are blocked in whites and others blocked in blacks. In general appearance, full-scale photographs show substance and texture throughout; underscaled look a little flat, overscaled look decidedly contrasty. Currently, overscaling dominates in photography.

Interestingly enough, when fidelity of reproduction is visualized, sensitometrist and zone-systemized craftsman take the same standards. At other times, they differ.

*Matching Negative Density Range to Paper Grade (Approximate)*

| Paper Grade | Density Range of Negative |
|:-----------:|:-------------------------:|
| 0 | 1.5 |
| 1 | 1.3 |
| 2 | 1.1 |
| 3 | .9 |
| 4 | .7 |
| 5 | .6 |

An example of *overscaled* would be Paper Grade 2 exposed to a negative range of 1.3 or 1.5.

An example of *underscaled* would be Paper Grade 2 exposed to a negative range of .7.

An example of *full scale* would be Paper Grade 2 exposed to negative range 1.1 or Paper Grade 4 exposed to negative range .7.

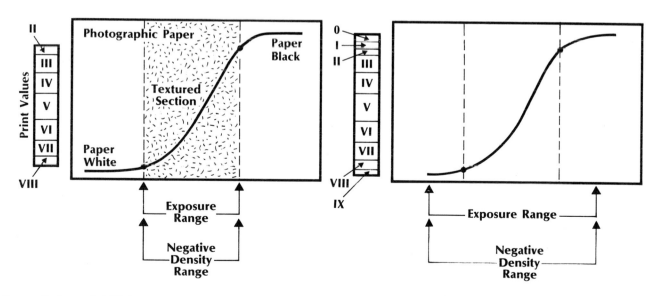

*Zones II through VIII for a textured print scale.*

*Zones 0 through IX for the full-scale print.* **103**

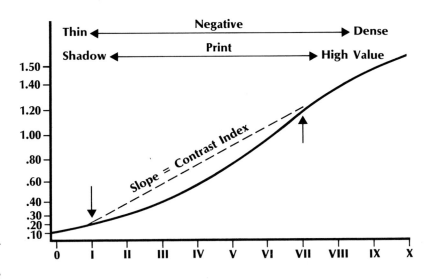

## Film Characteristics and the Visualization of Negatives

Working with film curves and negatives, we may again become aware of "movement" in the sensitometrist's D-log E curves. A sensitometrist will say offhandedly, "All sensitometric curves have the shape of an "S", but when he starts to be specific, he admits "That S is not fixed, believe me. Its shape will change when a paper or film is developed differently."

As a photographer also comes to feel that the S-curve has a life of its own, visualization from a curve begins to occur almost of its own accord.

The D-log E "S"'s for film negatives differ from paper positive curves in several ways profitable to the visualizing photographer.

**1.** The slope of a film curve is rarely as steep.

**2.** The film curve will accomodate a greater *input* of light. (Often 1000:1, as compared to Grade 0 paper, whose maximum is about 30:1.)

*Film speed is based on density 0.10 over base + fog (Zone I).*
*Developer contrast is indexed by the gradient (slope) of the mid-section.*

3. Film, being transparent, will produce a greater *output* (density range) than paper, which reflects light.
4. Speed Point is density 0.10 above base + fog (Zone I), not 0.60 above base + fog (Zone V).
5. Though the curves appear somewhat alike, one feature is reversed. The toe of the film curve correlates with shadow, not the high value—just the opposite of the paper curve.

Point 5 above requires more attention. Casual though it seems, it points to an essential of photography, namely the negative/positive characteristic. Up to now previsualization has been planned exclusively from the paper scale (zone ruler). For the first time now, we suggest *visualizing the negative during the period of previsualization.*

Film contrast is derived directly from the slope of the mid-section of the curve, paper contrast indirectly. For paper, contrast grade is determined by the exposure range (Scale Index). As the slope of the film and paper curves increases, so does the contrast, and conversely. For film, contrast is numerically specified as with a contrast index (gradient) number, for paper as a paper grade number.

During calibration many opportunities were presented for thinking from negative to print; every printing session is a fresh opportunity. Probably the reader has already looked at negatives enlarged on the easel, and tried to visualize the reversal that will soon take place in the developing tray. If not, it is a good exercise in visualization. Our experience indicates that sensitometric graphs, for some people, are an even better way of getting a good grip on visualizing both positive and negative at once. While this section unfolds toward such a union, we temporarily offer a visual device. Imagine that the part of the D-log E graph below the S-curve represents the negative, and the part above the curve represents the photographic print. Then the single line curve symbolizes negative and positive simultaneously.

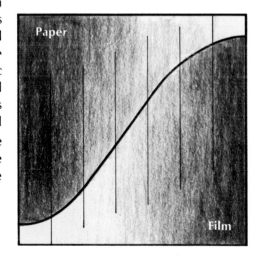

*Film and paper curves are here reversed and combined. (Symbolic)*

105

# Speed and Its Index

*The very first task of calibration was to find a new "working" speed index from a published rating*

The ASA speed point is related to that exposure which produces a density of 0.10 above film base + fog, for a very rigid, standard set of exposure and development conditions. By contrast, zone system speed determination is usually based on the same density of 0.10 above base + fog, *but for your own conditions of exposure, development, and printing.* The left hand figure illustrates three different films having speed values that are one-stop different. Note the displacement of the speed points along the exposure axis. As the speed point shifts to the right, more exposure is needed to obtain a density of 0.10 above base + fog. Therefore, the film has a lower speed number. As the speed point shifts to the left, less exposure is required because the film is faster, or more sensitive to light. Note well that the contrast is the same. This emphasizes that the speed differences among the films is in the films themselves, and not due to development changes.

However, for any single film, the speed point will shift somewhat with development. Consequently, *exposure compensations are necessary* for N+ and N− film development, as shown in the right hand illustration.

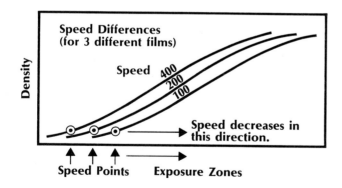

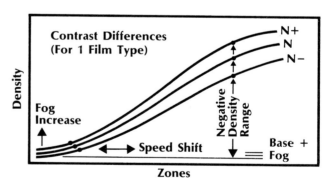

**Three Curves of Different Speeds and Identical Contrast**
*Films of one-stop speed differences, if developed identically would appear as shown. Note that the slopes are identical, thus contrasts of the negatives are the same. Like paper curves, film curves show speed shifts.*

**Three Curves Having Different Contrasts and Slightly Displaced Speed Points.**
*Speed point shifts slightly with changes of development. Exposure compensations are necessary for N+ and N− film development, as was demonstrated during Calibrations.*

## Contrast and Its Indexes

Contrast control by film development is derived from the gradient (slope) of a mid-section of the curve. Formerly the Greek word "gamma" was used to specify contrast.* Strictly, it is a mathematical measure of the "straight line portion" of the curve as it shifts from gentle to steep. However, few modern films (1975) have a "straight line" portion. Because of the multi-layering of films, the mid-section is curved, consequently the term gamma is disappearing. In place of gamma we have Contrast Index (Kodak) and Contrast Gradient (Ilford) to specify numerical estimates of contrast. The new terms are more relevant for practicing photographers because they measure the contrast in the film curves from about Zone I to about Zone VII.

Because of paper exposure scale limitations, film is normally developed to a contrast index of 0.60. This means that the density increase is only 60% of a given increase of log exposure. When contrast index is 1.00, the *density change in the negative is the same as the exposure change that produced it.* So we can truthfully say that as the gradient or its index changes, the local contrast of each zone changes.

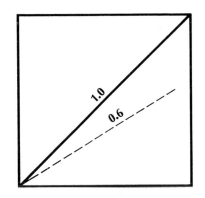

*Two ideal curves. The 45° angle curve (1.0) is ideal because the density change in the negative is the same as the exposure change that produced it. The 0.6 curve is ideal normal for the zone system because such a negative fits paper exposure scale limitations.*

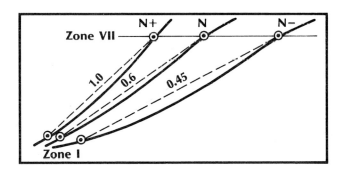

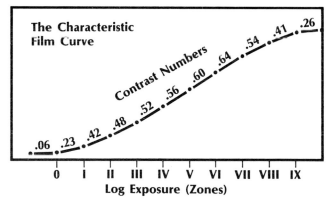

*Contrast gradients are derived as an average of the slope between Zone I and about Zone VII.*

*Note that the average line does not show the actual densities of the middle zones. Different developers will affect these middle zones differently.*

*See Appendix G

### Each Zone Has Its Own Slope of Contrast
*A D-log E curve can be visualized as a multiplicity of short curves, each having a slightly different gradient. In the curve above, the average slope between Zones I and VII is 0.56. That would be taken as the contrast index of the negative. It does not reveal the actual densities.*

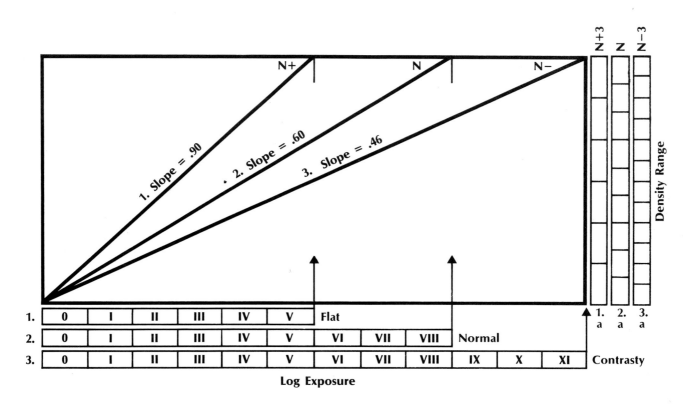

**Log Exposure**

## Summary of Contrast-Control by Film Development (Idealized)

*Films have been developed to three different gradients (contrasts) to accomodate three different subject brightness ranges, (1) flat, (2) normal, and (3) contrasty.*

*Imagine this graph as the top view of a billiard table. The billiard balls (Zones) are all bounced off the various angled slopes, and they all locate to the right in the positions shown.*

*Notice that although the overall density range is the same for all three scales, the **width** of each zone changes at the right. Adjusted by expansion to fit a flat scene (1a) there are fewer but wider zones. Compacted to adjust for a contrasty scene (3a) there are more but narrower zones.*

*Idealized diagrams emphasize at the expense of something. When visualizing, think of each zone as something elastic: proportions vary, "widths" fluctuate.*

# Deriving of Contrast Indexes from Densitometers and Published Data

To get at contrast control data stored in calibrated negatives and zone rulers is not simple. Laboriously matching certain zones, as if the photographer's zone rulers were a sensitometrist's D-log E curves, we can arrive at the development times and dilutions that we need. But, without a densitometer, no easy way offers itself for finding the contrast index of a calibration run. If the photographer has a densitometer available, approximate contrast indices for his or her calibration series can be found in the following manner:

Read the density of the exposure zone VII negative

Read the density of the exposure zone I negative

Subtract the Zone I density from the Zone VII density

Divide by 1.8

While the sensitometrist senses film development as affecting a change in negative density (increasing time increases density, decreasing time decreases density), zone system photographers sense film development as expansion and contraction **on either side of a norm.** As seen before, this "either side" concept extends to paper contrast grades.

Watching prints develop in the darkroom there is a unique opportunity to experience contrast, and empathize with its increase. The experience easily carries over to visualizing film development in the dark.

| Development | Density for VII | I | Zone VII minus Zone I | Divided by | Approximate Contrast Index |
|---|---|---|---|---|---|
| N+ (Expansion) | 1.25 | .15 | 1.10 | 1.8 | .61 |
| N (Normal) | 1.05 | .15 | .90 | 1.8 | .50 |
| N− (Compaction) | .85 | .15 | .70 | 1.8 | .39 |

If one is serious about plotting D-log E curves from densitometer readings of a calibration series, Appendix I carries directions.

Fortunately, manufacturers do publish development data in graph form—without reference to zones, of course. The information can provide a starting point whenever a new film is to be calibrated. There is an amazing amount of information present if one can read it. So learn to interpret the manufacturers' time-development curves. Directions appear in Appendix B.

The table above must be thought of as a guide line only. Films vary over wide ranges. Diffusion enlargers and condenser types are distinctly different light sources.

See appendix D.

Up to this point, photographer-readers may see little or no connection between these sensitometric curves and their photographs. We suspect that a visualization exercise may be in order.

1. Study the two photographs across the page for the distribution of their tonalities. As a hint, look for texture, or its absence, in the darks as well as the brights.
2. Which of the various sensitometric paper curves pictured below, correspond best; first to the upper picture, second to the lower picture.

*Film exposed so that Zone V is placed at III, V, and VII.*

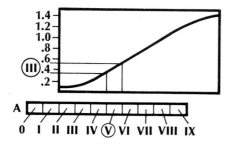

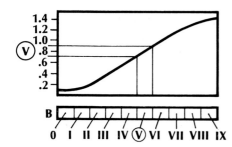

The visualization problem proposed in this exercise is neither obvious nor easy. Looking at the illustrations and imagining a single curve of a certain shape requires considerable information in order to make the connections. Fortunately, the photographer-reader has been exposed to the necessary information—and a little more is to come. Calibration work gave experience in connecting exposure and development to tonalities and their control; the opening illustration of the sensitometric section shows, by extension, a direct connection of zone rulers to these curves. So, see what you can do with the exercise.

Expect to spend a little time on the exercise; do not expect to be "successful" the first try. "Success" may come nearer the 100th attempt.

Photography does not do nearly enough to bring the scientist and the photographer together: photographers seem to be just as unwilling as the scientists, if not more so. Effort must be made on both sides, and individual photographers are not excluded. Attempting the exercise, is a step in the direction of understanding the scientific side of photography. It is a step that the photographer can make. And make to his or her benefit, by bringing "seeing" closer to the nature of the medium.

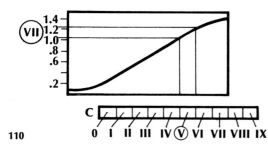

3. When there has been some "success" in visualizing photographic curves while looking at photographs; attempt the same visualizing from original subject to subsequent image.

Stevan Baron

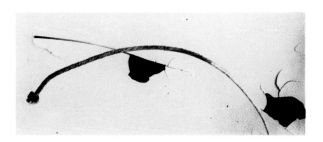

(Answer: Curves A or D provide best fit for top picture and Curve B for the bottom picture.)

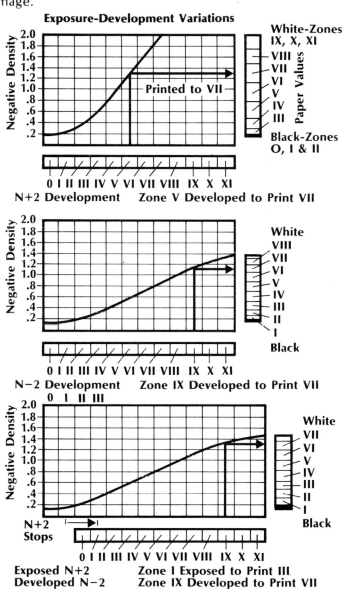

**Exposure-Development Variations**

Printed to VII

N+2 Development    Zone V Developed to Print VII

N−2 Development    Zone IX Developed to Print VII

Exposed N+2        Zone I Exposed to Print III
Developed N−2      Zone IX Developed to Print VII

111

# Zone Reproduction Cycle

After looking at the characteristics of film and paper separately, we can now turn to a study of how both work together to produce the photograph. Photographers and sensitometrists see the union differently. D-log E curves allow the latter to predict values of the print without actually making a photograph. The sensitometrist does this *graphically,* without light, by "exposing" one graph to another! (The photographer does it photographically, with light.) Further, we can graphically "expose" (combine) any one of a family of *film* curves with any one of a family of *paper* curves and predict the results of such a marriage. Or we can work in the opposite direction; by visualizing specific print values (child), we can then specify what characteristics the paper and the film (parents) need to have.

No doubt some explanations are in order.

Zone reproduction, or tone reproduction, involves tracing tonalities—in whatever form, values or zones—from subject through exposure, through negative and second exposure, into the final photograph. The Zone Reproduction *Cycle* involves the photographer's memory and imagination. The connecting link of the cycle is the photographer's power of visualization. What is learned from the first print is applied to the second; what is learned from the second is applied to the third, and so on, until the memory bank is filled. Thereafter knowledge is available for previsualization at a moment's notice.

We will (arbitrarily) start with the tonalities of the subject in diagramming the zone reproduction cycle. The photographer experiences the cycle in two phases, field and darkroom. To symbolize this gap in the creative process, the field phase appears on the adjoining page, and the darkroom phase overleaf. The sensitometrist's terms and scales are incorporated in both diagrams.

The same cycle is reproduced again on page 115 in somewhat simpler form. That diagram symbolizes an interim stage of the sensitometrist's grasp of the cycle as he focuses on the union of positive and negative. It is followed by a single graph which the sensitometrist equates with the photograph.

*Sensitometrists predict print values by exposing one graph to another. Photographers do the same with light.*

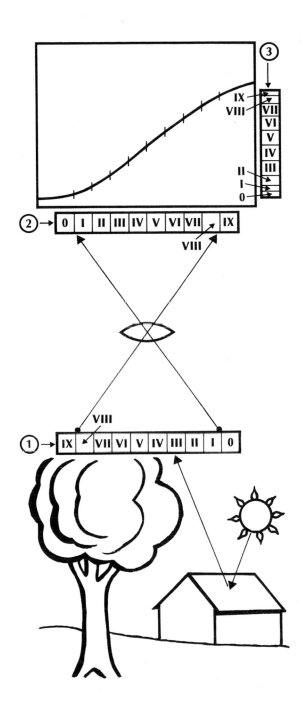

When the camera shutter is clicked, log luminance scale (1) of the scene becomes the log exposure scale (2) of the film. After the film is developed, negative density scale (3) is obtained. This scale is **elastic** and can be increased or decreased by N+ or N− development.

**Relationship of Photographic Scales (A)**

As a rule photographers experience the zone reproduction cycle in two phases, the first one is on location, the second while printing.

When the negative is exposed in an enlarger, the negative density scale (3) becomes the log exposure scale (4) for the paper. After the paper is developed, print densities (5) (print values) are obtained.
(Note the analogous function of camera and enlarger.)

**Relationship of Photographic Scales (B)**

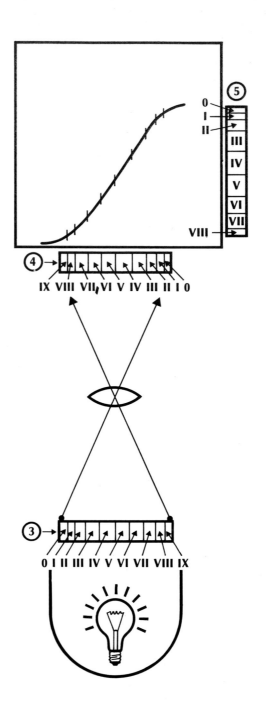

Since the photographer experiences the second phase in the darkroom the two phases tend to remain separate
The sensitometrist is not subject to this break in the creative cycle.

*By twisting the print zone scale on its side, the two-way flow becomes easily apparent. We can begin to see how the sensitometrist visualizes the whole cycle.*

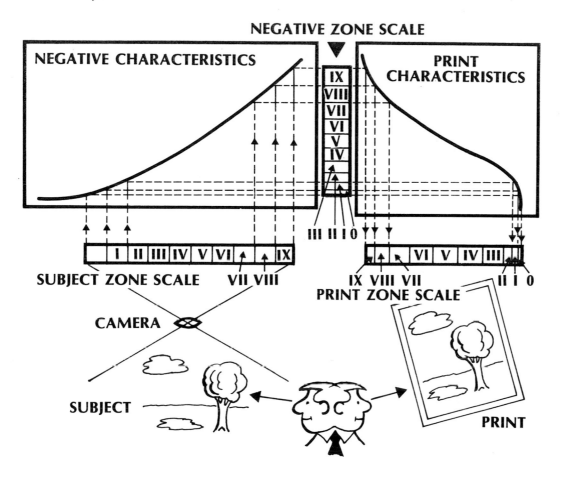

*The imagination of the photographer brings the zone reproduction cycle full circle.*

*A person completes the cycle with knowledge and imagination. Photographers work with light; they are physically aware of the succession of stages. Sensitometrists work with mathematics and visualize intellectually. We feel that when it comes to experiencing the union of negative and positive in a single photograph, the photographer can gain a new vision from the sensitometrist, and conversely.*

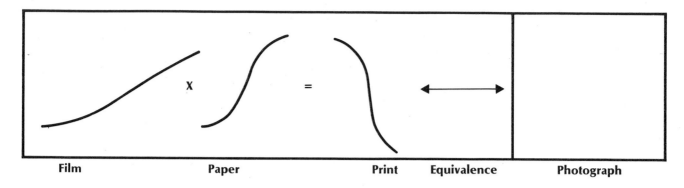

| Film | Paper | Print | Equivalence | Photograph |
|------|-------|-------|-------------|------------|

**Sensitometrists Visualize Negative and Positive Graphs**

## Graphic Representation of Sensitometric Visualization

Predicting zone contrast by "exposing" curve to curve, is simply a matter of multiplying the corresponding gradients of the film and paper curves. Knowing the slope of the film and paper curves for a given position or zone, a sensitometrist can predict the effect of the photographic process from subject values to print values. For example, the local contrast for *subject* values in Zone V will reproduce as *print* value V with a slope of 1.41: because the slope of the negative (0.60) multiplied by the slope of the print material (1.9) = 1.41. This slope is greater than 1.0; that means there is an increase in contrast. Therefore the tones in *print* value V will be a little more contrasty than they were in *subject* value V.

**Reproduction Slopes Arrived at Mathematically**

*The entire zone cycle then, may be, if one wishes, an exercise in visual thinking. Both the process, the "photo" and the graphical, if they are to resonate together, require some degree of sensitivity and understanding of how the photographic cycle can be manipulated and controlled.*

| Zones | | A<br>Film Slope<br>(Contrast) | B<br>Paper Slope<br>(Contrast) | A X B<br>Reproduction Slope<br>(Contrast) |
|-------|---|---|---|---|
| Shadows | I | .30 | .25 | .08 |
| | III | .54 | 1.5 | .81 |
| Mid-Section | V | .60 | 1.9 | 1.14 |
| | VII | .54 | 1.0 | .54 |
| High values | IX | .30 | .15 | .05 |

For a sensitometrist, visualization is plotting and drawing a graph that relates subject values to print values in *one* curve. It can be done only after going through the whole graphical zone reproduction cycle and finally replotting another S-shaped curve —but plotted as a reverse S. The reversed S means little to the layman but is highly significant to the sensitometrist: positive and negative are seen united in a single line. That single curve is the graphical equivalent of a photograph!

Photographers visualizing negative and positive simultaneously sense an interplay of zone rulers, though they may "see" no line.

**Photographers Visualize Positives and Negatives by Zone Rulers as symbolized below.**

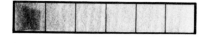

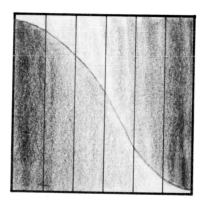

Steve Slesinger

# Shaping and Discovery: Putting It All Together

Depending on how the photographer-readers integrated their personal photography along with their injection of the zone system, a need may be present for our putting together again all this spate of information.

Being specific, do you recall the 6th and 7th steps of the procedural outline used to introduce the zone system? A statement was made then, that at this period in planning photographs, creative work could occur; and, except for picture editing, not much of anywhere else in the photographic process. At the place in the creative cycle associated with the 6th and 7th steps, visualization can be active, lively and effective. Considerable creative work occurs there, or can: meter reading, reading manipulations for sake of investigating options, mentally imagining different ways of rendering the subject, and best of all *discovering* how to manipulate the controls (tradeoffs) to achieve the rendering that, somehow during the creative work, was also discovered! Then crystalizing your discoveries with a series of directions; and following some of them, then and there, and the rest later in the darkroom.

The totality of all this active work and visualization suggests the creative activity associated with other artists, architects, and sculptors. Such activity also suggests what, not too long ago, was known as "the plastic problem." In fact Professor of Art, Graham Collier*, describes  two photo-pertinent aspects of this problem thus:

1. The plastic aspect, the *shaping* of two or three dimensions of some malleable material, be it paint which is brushed, marble which is carved, [latent image which is developed] to create the necessary form.

*Graham, Collier, *Art and the Creative Consciousness*, Prentice-Hall, New Jersey, 1972; page 3.

**2.** The expressive aspect, the *discovery* in and through the shaping process itself of the forms which will best emphasize the ideas and feeling present *in a state of heightened consciousness.* *(Italics ours.)

In photography the *plastic aspect* lies in the response of film and paper emulsions to light, as adjusted by exposure and development contrast control; implemented, of course, by zoned gray scales, standardized processing and calibrated zone rulers.

The *expressive aspect* lies in feeling and meter reading one's way among the picture possibilities, and discovering a plan for the future photograph. Or discovering how to print a certain negative, by virtue of having previsualized the possibilities in a state of heightened awareness, both at film exposure and at printing (previsualization and postvisualization).

When consciousness is keen and alert and awake, previsually thinking through any current plastic problem at interface becomes an active creative state. We do not necessarily mean ecstasy, in fact sometimes the ambience of creative thinking is one of struggle.

Perception researcher Professor Rudolf Arnheim, described visual thinking as a cognitive operation that includes, "active exploration, selection, grasping of essentials, simplification, abstraction, analysis and synthesis, completion, correction, comparison, problem solving, as well as combining, separation, putting into context." By cognitive he means, "all mental operations involved in the receiving and processing of information, sensory perception, memory, thinking, learning."*

No matter how much visual shaping must go on in a photographer's head, an analogy to molding clay can hardly be escaped. Rudolf Arnheim wrote in his *Visual Thinking,* "In looking at an object we reach out to it. With an invisible finger we move through the space around us, go out to distant places where things are found, touch them, catch them, scan their surfaces, trace their borders, explore their texture. It is an eminently active occupation."

We would add to all this a purpose: to live with a subject in resonance, to experience a scene for *what it is* by seeing *what else it is*—how many different photographs can be extracted from

* Rudolf Arnheim, *Visual Thinking,* Univ. of California Press, Berkeley, 1972; p 13.

*I don't take pictures, pictures take me. I can do nothing except have film in the camera and be alert. My adversary, a photograph, stalks the world like a roaring lion. One can only trust one's sensitivity, the bounty of the world, and the chemistry of Kodak. This is the photographic method.*
    Charles Harbut
    *(Travelog)*

*Zone System photographers, who can easily work as Harbut says, recognize something more in the photographic method: visualization.*

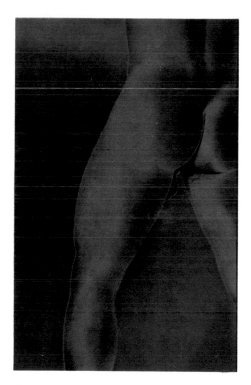

*The purpose of art is not to reproduce the visible, but to make visible.*
    Paul Klee

*Stieglitz put it "make visible the invisible."*

*I start with no preconceived idea—
discovery excites me to focus—
then rediscovery through the lens—
final form of presentation seen on ground
glass, the finished print previsioned
complete in every detail of texture, movement, proportion, before exposure—
the shutter's release automatically and
finally fixes my conception, allowing no
after manipulation—
the ultimate end, the print, is but a dupli-
cation of all that I saw and felt through
my camera.*

Weston

it. When such a purpose comes first, as we work, "revealing" photographs appear almost of their own accord, and in due time. "Revealing"; what does that mean here? Speaking metaphysically, it means uncovering our anti-ego Self in the subject. Next, encountering that part of the subject which is *not* any self in us. . . and so on. But such matters are too intangible for this book, so let us return to specifics.

Photographers' opportunities for "shaping" fall into three categories. (1) Which option or combination would best fulfill the desire to be a faithful witness of the subject or event (Reportive). (2) Which "shaping" would most clearly communicate the photographer's feeling about the subject (Expressive). (3) Which "shaping" would unmistakably reveal the fantasy-trip triggered by the view or scene (Subjective).

Awareness of so many possible combinations at interface puts the photographer on a par with the painter, so far as both are given many choices to work with, against, or in spite of. On the other side of the coin, multiple options may throw into confusion photographers who habitually defend the literal photograph, or any other idea of what a photograph should look like.

Now to a question much to the point. Were the photographers of the adjacent photographs using some form of zone system? Hazarding a guess is not good enough; do you know? If so, is it because of the photographer's reputation? Did you ever hear of any of them before? (Any viewer's notion that zone system pictures are always full of substance, whether it be fur, fins, flesh, or feathers, is of little help because sophisticated users of the system play the tonal options as if they were chords on a keyboard.) Yes, it is hard to tell which of the four persons used the system, if any did. Well-crafted prints appear by both plan and accident to the dismay of many. If being a systemized photographer is *not* obvious to friends and audiences, why continue with the system?

Any photographer who takes up the zone system expects to improve his or her camerawork. Such expectations are not unfounded; pictures that accord with his or her *intentions* are consistently produced. But that first surge of better quality levels off to a plateau sprinkled with bigger hills to climb than quality.

When we can make quality photographs consistently and

according to our intentions, we finally discover that any reason for continuing with the system comes from a desire to grow in wardly through *this* medium, not some other medium.

Such a reason beginners, of course, have no inkling of; but to continue for a lifetime with "tones and zones," product alone is not enough. The craft of photography must be added, and especially that aspect of craft which metaphysical ceramicists mean when they ask, "Which is the pot and which is the potter?"

If it is true that *natural* growth of body, mind and psyche slows to a stop at about age 20, and thereafter any inner growth is a matter of personal effort, we need to find some means of working at it. Any art or any craft can be a medium of inner growth. Still-photography *practiced as a medium* offers as many opportunities for inner evolution as pottery or weaving, film or drama, painting or music. A competent craftsman photographer can make a living with whatever form of photography he already practices. An advanced amateur can continue to exhibit without changing his style or techniques. Neither need such a concept as a zone system *until they want to attend to their inner development*. When learning turns from product, to shaping and discovering (craft) inner opening can start. Richard Boleslavski in his book *Acting: The First Six Lessons,* mentioned that a person could experience the birth of his or her soul through art.

# Appendices

## Appendix A

### Film Development Data: Six Films

The data originate in calibration runs made in accordance with the methods presented in this book. The films were Ilford Pan F, FP4, and HP4; Kodak Panatomic X, Plus-X, and Tri-X. All were developed in D-76 at 68°F with 30 seconds initial agitation, followed by 5 seconds of agitation every 30 seconds thereafter. The times given are for condenser enlargers, to print on a #2 contrast grade paper. For diffusion enlargers use the next higher grade of paper.

We publish this data with some hesitancy because of the rapid changes in photographic chemistry. Use it as a launching point for *personally* verified exposure-development data, just as you would any film manufacturer's published information.

These development times are based on roll film data, but may also be used as starting times for sheet film when developed by the tray method, using constant agitation. However when developing sheet film by the *tank* method with *intermittent* agitation, these times should be increased approximately 10%.

Regarding ASA ratings: when calibrating an unfamiliar film make it a rule to start testing at one-half the ASA rating (one stop more exposure). Why? Contemporary papers are not what they used to be and are changing fast. Although Zone I density of 0.1 (above base + fog) can be seen and measured in the negative, most contemporary enlarging papers cannot print it unless the Zone I density in the negative is doubled (to approximately 0.2). The film speeds published here for Normal development reflect this fact.

The Exposure Index compensations for N−2 and N+2 developments will maintain Zone I as a threshold black print value on normal (#2) contrast paper at standard print time with a condenser enlarger. Print on #3 grade paper with a diffusion enlarger. (See Appendix D)

**Low Speed Films**

| Exposure Index | Development Symbol | Time in Minutes | Developer Dilution |
|---|---|---|---|
| **Ilford Pan F** | | | |
| 12 | N−2 | 3½ 4½ | straight 1:1 |
| 18 | N−1 | 4½ 5½ | straight 1:1 |
| 25 | N | 6 10½ | 1:1 1:3 |
| 37 | N+1 | 6½ 10 | straight 1:1 |
| 50 Rated | N+2 | 9 13½ | straight 1:1 |
| **Panatomic X** | | | |
| 8 | N−2 | 3 4 | straight 1:1 |
| 12 | N−1 | 5 or 7 | straight 1:1 |
| 16 | N | 8 or 11 | 1:1 1:3 |
| 24 | N+1 | 9 or 11 | straight 1:1 |
| 32 Rated | N+2 | 13 or 15 | straight 1:1 |

Medium Speed Films

| | | | |
|---|---|---|---|
| **Ilford FP4** | | | |
| 30 | N−2 | 3½ or 5½ | straight 1:1 |
| 45 | N−1 | 4½ or 6 | straight 1:1 |
| 60 | N | 7 or 11 | 1:1 1:3 |
| 90 | N+1 | 8 or 10 | straight 1:1 |
| 125 Rated | N+2 | 11 | straight |

*Ilford FP4     68°     15 minutes     1:3*

| Exposure Index | Development Symbol | Time in Minutes | Developer Dilution |
|---|---|---|---|
| **Kodak Plus X** | | | |
| 30 | N−2 | 3½ 4½ | straight 1:1 |
| 45 | N−1 | 4½ or 6 | straight 1:1 |
| 60 | N | 7 or 10½ | 1:1 1:4 |
| 90 | N+1 | 7½ or 11 | straight 1:1 |
| 125 Rated | N+2 | 10½ 12 | straight |

High Speed Films

| Exposure Index | Development Symbol | Time in Minutes | Developer Dilution |
|---|---|---|---|
| **Ilford HP4** | | | |
| 100 | N−2 | 4 6½ | straight 1:1 |
| 150 | N−1 | 5½ or 9½ | straight 1:1 |
| 200 | N | 10½ or 12 | 1:1 1:2 |
| 300 | N+1 | 9 or 15 | straight 1:1 |
| 400 Rated | N+2 | 13 | straight |
| **Kodak Tri X** | | | |
| 100 | N−2 | 4½ 7½ | straight |
| 150 | N−1 | 6 or 8½ | straight 1:1 |
| 200 | N | 10 or 12 | 1:1 1:2 |
| 300 | N+1 | 11 or 14 | straight 1:1 |
| 400 Rated | N+2 | 14½ | straight |

# Appendix B

## Reading Mfgrs' Film Development Curves

The photographer can learn to estimate preliminary development times for calibration of an unfamiliar film from the maker's published curves. Several film manufacturers, including Kodak and Ilford, publish highly useful contrast control recommendations based on average gradient systems (slopes) for measuring the contrast of negatives. They are called Contrast-Time curves. Kodak's Contrast Index and Ilford's Average Gradient G (Gee-bar) are similar enough to use the published values of either to estimate the development times for a given negative contrast (N+1, N, N−2, etc.).

To read the contrast-time curves in zones one needs to know the correlation of zones to contrast gradients:

| Development Symbols | Contrast Gradients (G) |
|---|---|
| N+2 | 0.80-.85 |
| N+1 | 0.65-.70 |
| N | 0.50-.55 |
| N−1 | 0.45-.50 |
| N−2 | 0.35-.40 |

When starting to calibrate an unfamiliar film or developer refer to the table above, find the contrast gradient number for the development bracket ( ) you wish to test, then refer to the contrast-time curve. Locate the contrast gradient on the left, read across to the curve and down to minutes of development time. The graph on the next page is Ilford's contrast-time chart for FP4 and ID-11 (same as D-76). To make things simpler the Zone Correlates appear on the right and the contrast gradient numbers on the left.

These zone-to-contrast index (gradient) correlations hold generally. Consequently development data in zones can be read from any contrast-time curve. For example when one starts the expansion calibration, look up the N+1 G (contrast gradient) numbers in the table above. It is G 0.6-0.70. Find where the curve crosses this band and read development time in minutes at the bottom of the chart.

TAKE THESE TIMES AS A GUIDELINE! They are based on direct exposure to light, so they disregard the "in-camera" effects (flare mainly) Photographer's cannot escape.

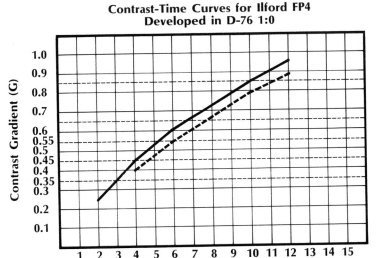

**Contrast-Time Curves for Ilford FP4
Developed in D-76 1:0**

Contrast Gradient (G)

Agitation:
- - - - Intermittent
——— Continuous

**Development Time in Minutes
The shaded bands cover variations in
films and developers**

*Ilford's contrast chart for FP4
and developer ID-11 (same as Kodak D-76).*

The correlations generally hold between zones and contrast indexes (contrast gradients). Here the zones have been added on the right to a published contrast-time curve.

The shaded bands cover the range of various films and development times.

Kodak publishes time-contrast data for most of its films, developed in D-76. (See *Kodak Black and White Films in Rolls,* Pamphlet AF13, and *Kodak Professional Black and White Films,* Data Book FS.)

Ilford also publishes time-contrast data for each of their films developed in ID-11 which is identical to Kodak D-76. (See Ilford Pamphlets A32.35 for FP4, A32.45 for HP4, and A32.2 for Pan F.)

## Mixing Manufacturers

When the photographer combines a developer made by X with a film made by Z he or she is on their own. The zone system calibration sequences are equal to the task they set for themselves.

**Summary Table for Appendices A & B**

**Sample Film: Tri-X or HP4**

| Exposure Compensation to Maintain Zone I at Threshold Black | | Estimated Average Gradient* or Contrast Index** Values | | Development Symbol |
|---|---|---|---|---|
| Sample Exposure Index | Exposure Change in Stops | Condenser Enlarger | Diffusion Enlarger | |
| 100 | +1 | 0.40 | 0.50 | N−2 |
| 150 | +½ | 0.45 | 0.55 | N−1 |
| 200 | None | 0.50 | 0.60 | N |
| 300 | −½ | 0.65 | 0.75 | N+1 |
| 400 | −1 | 0.80 | 0.90 | N+2 |

\* Ilford
\*\* Kodak
\*\*\* On normal contrast paper (#2 or #3) depending on brand and the photographer's preference.

# Appendix C

## Camera Flare and Darkroom Flare

*Manufacturers have all but eliminated flare from lenses, but not from cameras. Internal camera flare in even the best cameras can cause at least a one zone shift in the shadow area of the negatives. This is shown in the curve below.*

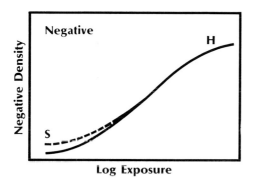

All optical systems (camera, enlarger—eyes *too*) cause light to be scattered within them. This non-image-forming light causes fog over the film or paper being exposed. The effect of flare is greatest in the shadow region of the negative; it is greatest in the high value region in the print. Flare, therefore, further decreases the already low slope in these regions. Unavoidable flare, though accounted for to some extent in zone calibration methods, still affects texture adversely in the shadows and brights. To help overcome the effect of flare is the reason that Zone III is placed just off of the toe of the negative curve, and that the film is developed so that Zone VII falls just below the shoulder.

Excessive flare can be avoided by keeping lenses clean, and filters free from dust and scratches and properly positioned, by using a lens hood, by taking precautions with back-lighted subjects, by properly masking the negative during printing, by avoiding long printing times if there is light scattered in the darkroom, by turning off the safelights during long printing times, and by painting darkroom walls a matte black.

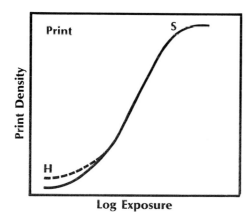

## Darkroom Flare Affects Highlight Densities

*Darkroom flare occurs while exposing paper to negatives. It comes from the scatter of light, and affects the highlight areas adversely as shown above.*

Safelights after several minutes can produce the effect of pre-exposure. (Such pre-exposure can be used for contrast-control when needed.)

## Flare Reduces Contrast in Shadows and Brights

*The effect of flare (dotted portion of the curves) is greatest where the density is least; in the negative the contrast loss is greatest in the shadow region (S), while in the print the loss is greatest in the high value region (H).*

# Appendix D

## Printing Difference Between Condenser and Diffusion Enlargers

The same negative printed with a condenser enlarger will have higher densities and contrast than if printed with a diffusion enlarger. This necessitates an increase in printing time and a change in paper grades.

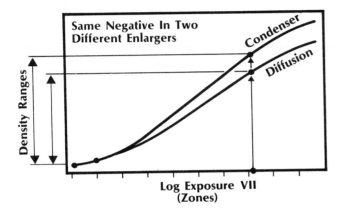

The reason for this is that the attenuation of light by the densities in a given negative is affected by the optical system in the enlarger. This is called the Callier Effect. For the same negative, the printing densities will be higher in a condenser-type enlarger than in a diffusion-type enlarger. Even changes from one make of enlarger to another, or among lenses on the same enlarger may require adjustment of the development time given the negative. Adjustment may also be required if films of quite different speeds are used since high-speed films tend to have coarse grains which scatter more light than fine grain slow-speed films.

# Appendix E

## Reciprocity Effects

All light-sensitive emulsions are subject to reciprocity effects. Interestingly enough, even the retina of the eye experiences the effect, desert noon light for example. When film or paper is èxposed at extremely short or long times, adverse reciprocity effects occur. To offset this requires an adjustment in exposure and sometimes also in development.

The term reciprocity suggests that something is related to something else in a special way. In photography, the two variables that make up exposure—light and time—are indeed reciprocal. An exposure of 100 units of light for 1/10 of a second is the same as an exposure of 10 units of light for 1 second. In each case, the exposure is 10; the units of light and the time are reciprocal. However, when exposures run very long or short, the photographic effect—density—will "fall off," even though the two exposures are equivalent. The reciprocity effect works two ways, *for* and *against* the picture maker.

### Film Reciprocity

Fortunately, for most pictorial films, reciprocity is of no consequence over quite a wide range of exposure times. Only at extremely short (less than about 1/1000 sec) or long (more than about 1 second) exposure times, must adjustments be made. Notice from the table on the next page that both camera exposure and film development must be adjusted.

## Reciprocity Data for Film

The manufacturer suggests, "The photographer should use the exposure adjustment given in the tables as a mid-point in bracketing his exposures when lighting conditions are such that reciprocity effects may be encountered." (Note that more of an increase is needed to adjust for reciprocity if exposure time is used rather than f-stops.) The data will serve as a starting point for other films.

## Kodak Professional Black-and-White Films— Reciprocity-Effect Adjustments

### Kodak Film

EKTAPAN 4162 (ESTAR Thick Base)*
PANATOMIC-X
PLUS-X Pan
PLUS-X Pan Professional
PLUS-X Pan Professional 2147 (ESTAR Base)
PLUS-X Pan Professional 4147 (ESTAR Thick Base)
PLUS-X Portrait 5067

ROYAL Pan 4141 (ESTAR Thick Base)
ROYAL-X Pan 4166 (ESTAR Thick Base)
ROYAL-X Pan
SUPER-XX Pan 4142 (ESTAR Thick Base)
TRI-X Pan
TRI-X Pan Professional
TRI-X Pan Professional 4164 (ESTAR Thick Base)

### Use

| If Indicated Exposure Time Is (seconds) | Either This Lens Aperture Adjustment | Or This Exposure Time Adjustment (seconds) | And in Either Case, Use This Development Adjustment |
|---|---|---|---|
| 1/1000 | None | None | 10% more |
| 1/100 | None | None | None |
| 1/10 | None | None | None |
| 1 | 1 stop more | 2 | 10% less |
| 10 | 2 stops more | 50 | 20% less |
| 100 | 3 stops more | 1200 | 30% less |

* KODAK EKTAPAN Film 4162 (ESTAR Thick Base) does not require a development time adjustment for exposures of 1/1000 second.

### Kodak Film

Commercial 4127 (ESTAR Thick Base)
Commercial 6127

### Use

| If Indicated Exposure Time Is (seconds) | Either This Lens Aperture Adjustment | Or This Exposure Time Adjustment (seconds) | And in Either Case, Use This Development Adjustment |
|---|---|---|---|
| 1/100 | None | None | 10% more |
| 1/25 | None | None | None |
| 1/10 | None | None | 10% less |
| 1 | None | None | 20% less |
| 10 | 1/2 stop more | 15 | 30% less |
| 100 | 1 stop more | 300 | 40% less |

Kodak Publication No. 0-2/1971

Reproduced by courtesy of Kodak-at-Rochester.

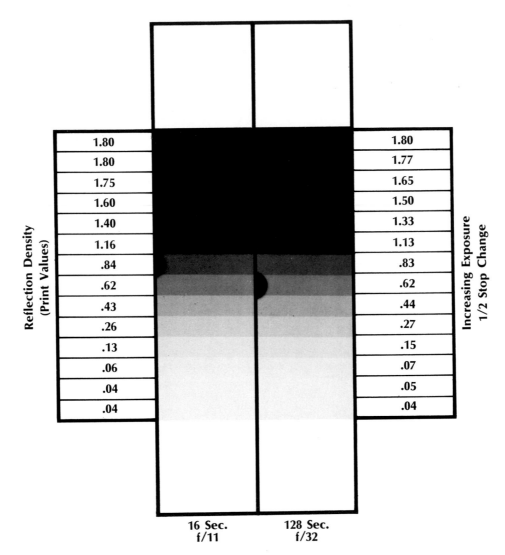

| Reflection Density (Print Values) | | 16 Sec. f/11 | 128 Sec. f/32 | | Increasing Exposure 1/2 Stop Change |
|---|---|---|---|---|---|
| 1.80 | | | | 1.80 | |
| 1.80 | | | | 1.77 | |
| 1.75 | | | | 1.65 | |
| 1.60 | | | | 1.50 | |
| 1.40 | | | | 1.33 | |
| 1.16 | | | | 1.13 | |
| .84 | | | | .83 | |
| .62 | | | | .62 | |
| .43 | | | | .44 | |
| .26 | | | | .27 | |
| .13 | | | | .15 | |
| .06 | | | | .07 | |
| .04 | | | | .05 | |
| .04 | | | | .04 | |

### Reciprocity Effect in Paper

*Both strips received the same equivalent exposures but at different exposure times. The results, however, are not equivalent and the difference can be estimated by comparing the displacement for a middle gray value. Each step represents 1/2 stop change in exposure. For this particular photographic paper, a middle gray value of .84 density at 16 seconds is used as a reference point. Assume that it represents a Print Value of V. When the same paper is given an equivalent exposure at 128 seconds, there is a 1/2 stop speed loss which renders Print Value V as a density of 0.62. To adjust for this, as least a 1/2 stop increase in exposure is required. This is approximated above by simply moving the test strip 1/2 stop. This speed loss and contrast change in the darker Print Values is the reciprocity effect—same equivalent exposures but different Print Values.*

## Paper Reciprocity

Not much published reciprocity data are available for papers, so you will have to generate your own. This is easily done by buying a Kodak Number 2 step wedge and running an exposure series in contact with a piece of photographic paper. Use times like 8, 16, 32, 64, 128 seconds. *Vary the f-stops so that the exposures are equivalent.* The Kodak wedge is stepped off in ½-stops so you can, by matching the gray areas in the print, determine what exposure adjustments are necessary when excessive exposure times are used. The marked step in the adjacent figure approximates a Print Value V. When a given paper is exposed at 16 seconds and a second piece is given an equivalent exposure at 128 seconds, there is a ½-stop speed loss which renders Print Value V as a lower density of 0.62.

# Appendix F

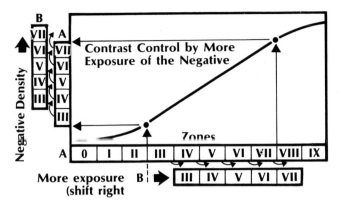

*One stop more exposure shifts the entire Exposure Scale one zone to the right and shifts the entire Density Scale one value darker. Negative density scale B compared to A shows that contrast is increased in the shadow areas but decreased in the highlight areas.*

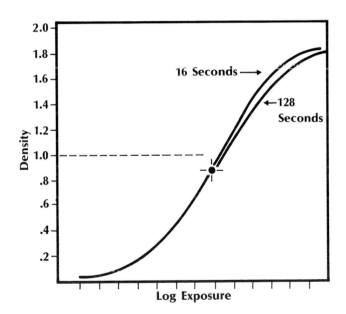

## Paper D-log E Curve Showing Reciprocity Effect

*The 128-second curve has been shifted 1/2 stop to the left so that it coincides with the 16 second curve at a print density of 0.84. Note that there is no change in contrast for Print Values lower than 1.0 density but a lowering of contrast for the darker Print Values above a 1.0 density level.*

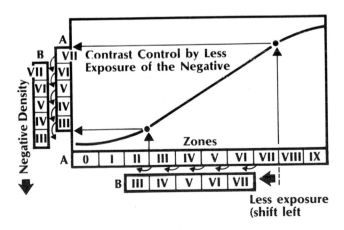

*One stop less exposure shifts the entire Exposure Scale one zone to the left and shifts the entire Density Scale one value lighter. Negative density scale B compared to A shows that contrast is increased in the highlight areas but severely decreased in the shadow areas.* **129**

# Appendix G

## Slope and Contrast

The slope or incline of a curve describes its potential contrast. Slope is a measure of the *rate* that output changes as a function of input. In photography, it is the rate at which density increases as a function of increasing exposure. The D-log E curve is a rate curve.

The following sequence is intended as a review of how slope is measured. We will use a two-inch square for our sequence.

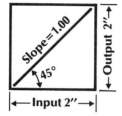

### 1. Slope =1.0

Divide a 2″ square, or any square as shown, and you produce a slanted line that can be called an incline or a slope. Since it is at an angle of 45°, it has a slope of 1.0. You can show this mathematically:

$$\text{Slope} = \frac{\text{OUTPUT}}{\text{INPUT}} = \frac{2}{2} = 1.0$$

(Mathematicians will recognize that the tangent of an angle $= \dfrac{\text{opposite}}{\text{adjacent}}$ and that the Tan 45° = 1.0.)

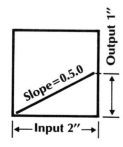

### 2. Slope = 0.50

The slope or curve for this relationship is less than one because output is less than input.

$$\text{Slope} = \frac{\text{OUTPUT}}{\text{INPUT}} = \frac{1}{2} = 0.50 \text{ or } 50\%$$

This means the output has been reduced to 50% of the input. In photography a gamma of 0.50 means the same thing. The *rate* of increase of density is only 50% of the exposure given.

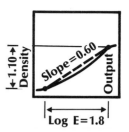

### 3. Photographic Curve

Note that for a photographic material, the curve is not a straight line. We can, however, draw a straight line as an average between two select points on the curve (useful shadows and highlights). The input is Log Exposure and output is Density.

To find the average slope, use the same formula:

$$\text{Slope} = \frac{\text{OUTPUT}}{\text{INPUT}} = \frac{\text{Density range}}{\text{Log E range}} = \frac{1.1}{1.8} = 0.60$$

Depending on how the two select points are located on the curve, the slope is called *contrast index* or *average gradient*. If the curve were a straight line, it would be called *gamma*.

In zone system nomenclature, the slope of the D-log E curve between III and VII provides the best contrast and is sometimes referred to as the texture region.

# Appendix H

## Glossy and Matte Surfaces Compared

*Glossy surfaces reach a maximum-density black of about 1.90, while matte surfaces reach only about 1.60. Other surfaces, such as luster or semi-matte, will give maximum black densities somewhere between 1.60 and 1.90.*

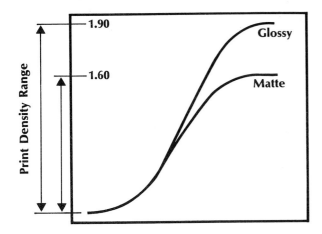

# Appendix I

## Calibration with Densitometer and Graphs

Commercial calibrated step wedges can be used for film exposure in these tests. It is faster, but it also bypasses the integration of equipment, processing habits, flare effect and so on associated with doing the test through your camera. Below the *entire* calibration process is telescoped and specially modified for extracting data with densitometer and D-log E curves.

Preparation: As given starting page 52, except use the 18% gray neutral test card exclusively. Have shutters checked without fail and use their current speeds.

Have lens stops checked with equal care.

Exposure: *Roll Film.* Expose Zones 0 through XI one frame at a time.
        *Sheet Film.* Make three exposures per sheet according to schedule in adjacent column.

The sample exposures were chosen to avoid reciprocity fall-off. It is based on a Zone V placement of the 18% test card on a bright day in the sun.

Development: The four sheets of film make up one set. Six such sets are required. Assuming manufacturer recommends 8-10 minutes development, bracket by developing one set at each time: 4, 6, 8, 10, 14 and 20 minutes. (Six sets are sufficient for preliminary curve plotting. Additional sets for the odd-numbered minutes might be added for more information. Extend to 40 minutes if extensive expansions are being investigated.)

Density Readings: On the densitometer, actually read only the center of the negative, to avoid any uneven illumination or development effects. Take several readings within a small central area and average them.

### Multiple Exposure Schedule for Sheet Film

|  |  |  | Sample Exposure | |
|---|---|---|---|---|
| | Zone 0 | Insert dark slide 1/3 way in. | (No Exposure) | |
| Sheet A | Zone I | Expose for Zone I Move slide 2/3 in. | f/45 | 1/30 |
| | Zone II | Repeat Zone I exposure | f/45 | 1/30 |
| | Zone III | Dark slide out Expose for III | f/22 | 1/30 |
| Sheet B | Zone IV | Slide in 1/3 Repeat exposure for III | f/22 | 1/30 |
| | Zone V | Slide in 2/3 Double exposure for III | f/16 | 1/30 |
| | Zone VI | Dark slide out Expose for VI | f/8 | 1/30 |
| Sheet C | Zone VII | Slide in 1/3 Repeat exposure for VI | f/8 | 1/30 |
| | Zone VIII | Slide in 2/3 Double exposure for VI | f/5.6 | 1/30 |
| | Zone IX | Dark slide out Expose for IX | f/8 | 1/30 |
| Sheet D | Zone X | Slide in 1/3 Repeat exposure for IX | f/8 | 1/30 |
| | Zone XI | Slide in 2/3 Double exposure for IX | f/5.6 | 1/30 |

*For maximum accuracy expose on one sheet per zone. Process Zone 0 with the rest. Use ample or even excessive amounts of developer, otherwise exhaustion can distort the densities.*

**Plotting a D-log E Curve.**

**1.** Use a sheet of graph paper to prepare vertical and horizontal scales as shown to the right. The spacing should be the same for both scales.

**2.** Label the horizontal scale "Relative Camera Exposure Scale" and the vertical scale "Density Scale." Mark both off in equal increments as shown.

**3.** Number the vertical density scale as shown. Roman numeral the horizontal scale. This establishes the Zones. Density scale and Exposure Zone scale now have corresponding I stop increments.

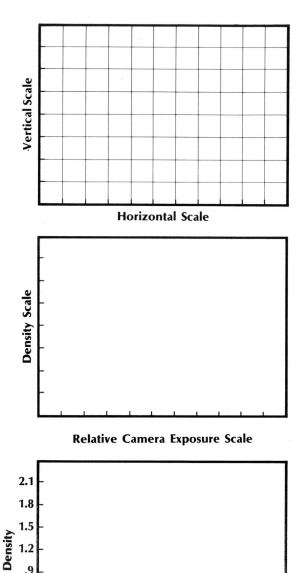

Horizontal Scale

Relative Camera Exposure Scale

**4.** Read the densities of your *normal* development set. For each exposure-density pair plot an intersect point.

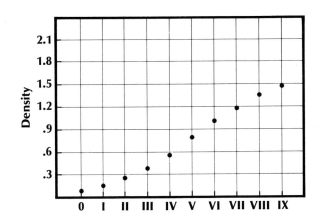

**5.** Join the points into a smooth curve. It now describes the characteristic of the film for the given development.

You now have a curve describing the relationship between exposure and density, between input and output, between stimulus and response.

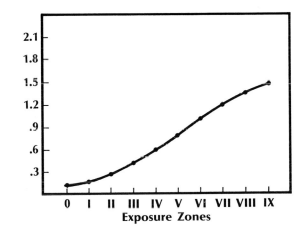

**6.** Plot the densities for the remainder of the negatives in sets as they were exposed. Smooth out the curves for each developing time. Add development time at the ends of each curve.

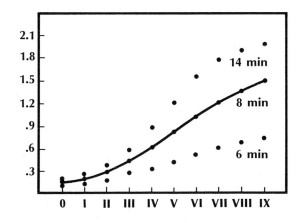

133

Now you can determine the various development brackets, N, N+, N−.

**7.** To determine Normal, draw a line horizontally from between density 1.15 and 1.2. Draw another line vertically from Zone VII exposure. Temporarily take the curve closest to where these two lines intersect as Normal.

A line drawn vertically from Zone V that intersects this curve at about density .75 will strengthen the case for this curve. Note its development time.

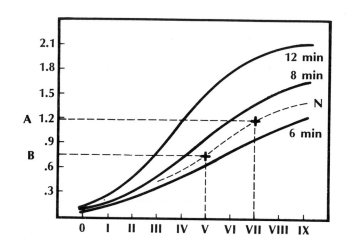

**A** Zone VII at 1.2 falls between the 8 and 6 minute curves, so 7 minutes is taken as a trial Normal.

**B** ZONE V at .75 on the 7 minute curve nicely, thus strengthening the possibility that the 7 minute curve will prove to be Normal.

**8.** To find N+1, observe which curve is closest when Zone VII exposure intersects a horizontal line at density 1.35 (Zone VIII). To find N−1 observe the event when Zone VIII exposure intersects density 0.95, and so on. The table of zones and densities to the right indicates rough correlations of negative densities to zones.

## Negative Densities Correlated with Zones

| Zone | 4 x 5 | 120 | 35mm | Description |
|------|-------|-----|------|-------------|
| 0 | fbf | fbf | fbf | film base + fog Maximum Black |
| I | .15 | .15 | .15 | Almost Dark |
| II | .30 | .28 | .25 | Very Black |
| III | .45 | .40 | .35 | Gray-Black |
| IV | .60 | .55 | .50 | Dark Gray |
| V | .75 | .70 | .65 | Middle Gray |
| VI | .90 | .85 | .80 | Light Gray |
| VII | 1.05 | 1.00 | .95 | Lighter Gray |
| VIII | 1.20 | 1.15 | 1.10 | Almost White |
| IX | 1.35 | 1.30 | 1.25 | White |

**Density Numbers Will Vary**

Density numbers given are all above film base plus fog (fbf). These densities are for condenser-type enlargers. For diffusion-type enlargers use either the next highest paper grade or Zone VIII density for Zone VII and Zone VI density for Zone V. Zone 1 (speed point) remains the same.

Please remember that these density numbers were derived under a specific set of conditions. The density number you derive may vary somewhat depending upon such things as the film used (fine grain vs moderate grain film), the type of densitometer and the type of film developer.

To obtain better separation between Zones 0 and I with the photographic papers currently in use it is preferable to aim for a density of 0.15 above film base plus fog for Zone I than the traditional 0.10.

Think of the specific numbers as the middle of the correlated zones. Density 0.75 for Zone V should be understood as a *band* between VI and IV. Realize also that the zones of negatives have considerable flexibility by virtue of paper grade contrast controls and variable exposure. Adams says they "really are zones."

When development times have been editorially assigned to N−2 to N+2, try them out. Painstakingly meter and record a scene that fits Normal development, expose and develop according to your estimated Normal time, print standard and check results OR do an establishing run on one sheet of film exposed to Zones I, V, and VII (or VIII or IX as you wish). Read the dried negatives and check against the table on the previous page. If Zone I is too high or low adjust Exposure Index for the second run. If the VII reading is more than half a zone off either way, adjust development time accordingly and test again.

# Appendix J

### A Brief History of the Zone System

Early photographers seem to have developed a sixth sense for exposure time in the field and film development time under red light. A few successes kept their enthusiasm alive.

The early photographers were less enthused regarding the attempts in 1890 of Ferdinand Hurter and Vero Driffield to bring order into their chaotic, hit-or-miss, rule-of-thumb state of photography. These two scientists had hoped to make photography easier for practicing photographers, but the men with the cameras did not think that H & D's science and numbers would be useful. They feared that the science would remove the spontaneity from the art, or that they would have to become scientists to work the system. Thus, the same complaint today leveled at the zone system, goes all the way back to Hurter and Driffield and the earliest beginnings of a discipline for an art medium within photography. While the photographers of their day

shied away from their good intentions, the manufacturers took them seriously. Look what manufacturers and scientists have done for the millions who still think that science and numbers are of little importance to their snapshots. The technology has been so refined that children of all ages can do photography.

Advanced thinkers though they were, Hurter and Driffield were too early to see how to marry the art and science of photography. They dreamed of perfect negatives and perfect prints. The opening statement of their report on the "H & D Curve" in the *Journal of the Society of Chemical Industry* (1890) is classic: "The production of a perfect picture by means of photography is an Art. The production of a technically perfect negative is a science." Today we like to think we are a little more sophisticated than that. So far as we understand that the most useful negative is one conditioned by the purposes and intentions of the photographer, we do not get caught in the trap of standardized "perfection". However many critics, curators and photographers still cling to the H & D notion of perfection. They do so in spite of recent sensitometry codifications that re-emphasize the significance of the photographer's intentions to use the negative as a step toward a fine, well-crafted, and expressive print.

Following the appearance of the electric luminance meters, as early as 1932 in Europe and America, more than one codification of sensitometry was attempted for the expressive and professional photographer.

In an article, "Weston Emulsion Speed Ratings,"[*] meter inventor and Vice President of the Weston Electrical Instrument Company, W.N. Goodwin, Jr., explained how the Weston meter could be used to predetermine densities in negatives. In 1938 H.P. Rockwell, Jr., of the same company, addressed the Fourth Annual Convention of the Photographic Society of America at Rochester, New York.[**] Under the title "Exposure Makes the Picture" he briefly showed the mathematical relationship between scene brightness range, negative development, and density ranges of printing papers. He emphasized subject contrast control by exposure rather than by variable development of the negative. Nevertheless he offered *a workable system of variable development based on a coordination of subject contrast*

[*] American Photography, 1935
[**] Pamphlet: Weston Electrical Instrument Corp.

and gamma gradients. John L. Davenport, a chemical engineer and an advanced amateur photographer published a two-part article titled, "Constant Quality Prints."*** Using Weston Meter Model 650, he demonstrated a method whereby the brightest and darkest parts of a scene could be measured and translated into film development times for producing uniform negatives. He said this about the dials of the Weston exposure meter, "They are placed there for the purpose of having the photographer always think of his subjects in terms of brightness range. It is one of the most important conceptions in photography and has been neglected too long."

At the same time (1939-40) Ansel Adams and Fred Archer, teaching photography at the Los Angeles Art Center School, were doing similar research. They were acquainted with the Davenport articles and the Hurter and Driffield report. They extended Davenport's method into a less mathematical and more visual one. In equating "stop" with "zone" they established a ten-zone visual print scale for black-and-white photography, Zones 0 through IX. The first publication was Adams' *Exposure Record*, 1945. In a letter (Summer 1974) Adams wrote; "It was after the Art Center School experience that the full impact of the zone system in relation to visualization was revealed to me." Previsualization was, of course, the feature that Goodwin, Rockwell, and Davenport lacked. The demise of the Weston Electrical Instrument Company in 1974 will be regreted for a long time to come by those who love the craft of photography.

***U.S. Camera, Nos. 12 & 13, 1940.

# Appendix K

### Selenium Toning for Black Intensification

Several photographic papers respond to selenium toning by approximately a one zone darkening of the blacks. Since the whites are not noticeably affected, the results amount to an increase of contrast.

The following formula prevents the color from reaching its customary browns; so along with the darkening of the blacks goes a slight change of color toward a rich purple brown that varies with the brand of paper. Since the effect of both darkening and color change is subtle, keep a wet untoned print close by for compari-

### Schedule and Formulas

| | | |
|---|---|---|
| First Fixer | ½ recommended time | |
| Wash | running water | 5-30 minutes |
| Second Fixer | (Mixed without hardener) | 2-5 minutes |
| (No rinse or wash) | | |
| Selenium Toner | (80°) | 3-7i minutes |
|   Water | 3,000 cc | |
|   Hypo Clear (Kodak) | 800 cc stock | |
|   Rapid Selenium Toner (Kodak) | 100 cc | |
|   Water to make | 4,000 cc | |
| Wash (running water) | | 6 minutes |
| HE1 (Kodak) for Archival processing | | 6 minutes |
| Wash (Kodak) for Archival processing | | 30-60 minutes |

son while toning. Tone it after the others are in the wash.

Toning varies from brand to brand, and batch to batch, so frequent testing is necessary. Increase or decrease the amount of toner: 50cc, 200cc, 300cc, and so on, per gallon. Water supply sometimes causes pronounced staining. In such an event try adding 3% ammonia to the toner: 50cc, 100cc, 150cc, etc. per gallon. Filtering the water supply may also be necessary.

Fresh toner will act in 3 minutes; use the same solution until 7 minutes are required to produce the desired effect. Then discard.

The coating effect of the selenium on the silver grains improves the archival properties.

# References

Adams, Ansel
**Camera and Lens,** 1971
**The Negative,** 1972
**The Print,** 1971
**Natural-Light Photography 1971**
**Pocket Exposure Record,** 1973 Edition
Dobbs Ferry, N.Y.
Morgan & Morgan

American National Standards Institute
1430 Broadway
N.Y., N.Y. 10018
PH 2.5-1972 "Method for determining speed of photographic negative materials (monochrome, continuous-tone)"
PH 2.17-1958 "Diffuse reflection density"
PH 2.19-1959 "Diffuse transmission density (ISO R5)"
PH 2.25-1965 "Photographic printing density"
PH 3.49-1971 "General-purpose photographic exposure meters"

Arnheim, Rudolf
**Visual Thinking**
Berkeley, Los Angeles, London
University of Calif. Press, 1974

Colller, Graham
**Art and the Creative Consciousness**
New Jersey
Prentice-Hall, 1972

Davis, Phil
**Photography**
Dubuque, Iowa
Wm. C. Brown, 1975

Dowdell, J.J. and Zakia, R.D.
**Zone Systemizer**
Dobbs Ferry, N. Y.
Morgan & Morgan, 1974

Dunn, J. F. & Wakefield, G. L.
**Exposure Manual**
Dobbs Ferry, N.Y.
Morgan & Morgan, 1974

Ferguson, W.B. (ed.)
**The Photographic Researches of Ferdinand Hurter and Viro C. Driffield**
Dobbs Ferry, N.Y.
Morgan & Morgan, 1974

**Focal Encyclopedia of Photography, The**
(Desk edition) New York
McGraw-Hill, 1969

Gassan, A.
**Handbook for Contemporary Photography**
Athens, Ohio
Handbook Co., 1974

**Kodak Data Books**
Kodak Professional Black-and-White Films
Kodak B/W Photographic Papers
Halftone Methods for the Graphic Arts

Morgan, D.O., Vestal, D., Broecker, W.L.
**Leica Manual**
Dobbs Ferry, N.Y.
Morgan & Morgan, 1973

Neblette, C.B.
**Fundamentals of Photography,** 1970
**Photography, Its Materials and Processes,** 1962
New York
D. Van Nostrand Co.

Newhall, Beaumont
**The History of Photography**
New York
Doubleday & Co., 1964

Stroebel, L. and Todd, H.N.
**Dictionary of Contemporary Photography**
Dobbs Ferry,N.Y.
Morgan & Morgan, 1974

Swedlund, Charles
**Photography**
New York
Holt, Rinehart & Winston, Inc., 1974

Time-Life (ed.)
**Light and Film**
New York
Time-Life Books, 1972

Todd, H.N. and Zakia, R.D.
**Photographic Sensitometry**
Dobbs Ferry, N.Y.
Morgan & Morgan, 1974

Upton, J. & Upton, B.
**Photography**
Boston
Little Brown, 1976

Vestal, David
**Craft of Photography**
New York, London
Harper & Row, 1975

Zakia, R.D.
**Perception & Photography**
Englewood Cliffs, N.J.
Prentice-Hall, 1975

# Subject Index

**Minor White** received his degree in botany from the University of Minnesota before turning to his career in photography. He studied the Zone System and began teaching with Ansel Adams in 1946 at what is now the San Francisco Art Institute. He taught at the Rochester Institute of Technology and the Massachusetts Institute of Technology as Professor of Creative Photography. Professor White was one of the leading experts on the Zone System. In 1953 he wrote the first version of the *Zone System Manual* for *Aperture,* the renowned quarterly of photography. He was an active photographer whose work is exhibited in major museums and galleries around the world.

**Richard Zakia** is concerned with and interested in facilitating the transfer of knowledge from sensitometry and visual perception to the making of photographs. He received a degree in photographic science from the Rochester Institute of Technology, and a doctorate in educational psychology from the University of Rochester. He has worked as a photographic engineer with the Eastman Kodak Company and is presently professor of Photography, School of Photographic Art and Science at R.I.T. Dr. Zakia is author of the book, *Perception and Photography,* and co-author, with Hollis Todd, of the books, *Photographic Sensitometry, 101 Experiments in Photography, Color Primer I & II,* and with John Dowdell, *The Zone Systemizer.*

**Peter Lorenz** was born in St. Louis, Missouri, where he took his degree in psychology at Washington University. While doing graduate work at Tufts University in 1967, he became involved in photography with Lee Parks at the Massachusetts Institute of Technology. In 1970, he began teaching the Zone System at the photography lab called *Zone V.* He is presently a teacher at the New England School of Photography in Boston and conducts free lance workshops on the Zone System.